D0180404

THE
QUEST
FOR THE
MALE
SOUL

THE QUEST FOR THE MALE SOUL

IN SEARCH OF SOMETHING MORE

MARTIN PABLE, CAPUCHIN

AVE MARIA PRESS NOTRE DAME, INDIANA 46556

International Standard Book Number: 0-87793-580-7

Cover and text design by Katherine Robinson Coleman

Printed and bound in the United States of America.

Library of Congress Cataloging-in-Publication Data

Pable, Martin W.
        The quest for the male soul : in search of something more / Martin W. Pable.
            p.   cm.
        Includes bibliographical references
        ISBN 0-87793-580-7
            1.   Men (Christian theology)   2.   Masculinity (Psychology)—Religious aspects—Christianity. 3. Men—Religious life. 4. Christian life—Catholic authors.   I. Title.
        BT703.5.P33 1996
        248.8'42—dc20
                                                        96-31129
                                                        CIP

Contents

PREFACE

About ten years ago I was assigned to full-time retreat work in Saginaw, Michigan. For the first few months I was bored. We were intensely busy during the weekend retreats, but the rest of the week I had too much time on my hands. I wasn't used to that.

During Christmas break I went back to Wisconsin and told my good friends Dick and Margie Schwebel about my discontent. Their response caught me off guard: "Why don't you write a book?" I had told myself a long time ago that I would write only if two conditions were present. First, there was little or nothing already written about a certain topic (why should I add another dish to an already full menu?). And second, the topic would have to be something I have direct knowledge of and feel deeply about.

When I shared this with Dick and Margie, they said, "Well, why not write about your experiences with men on retreats?" It was the obvious question. For several years I had been conducting retreats for men in Racine, Wisconsin, and had formed a support group for men who were trying to deepen their spiritual life. (They called themselves "Marty's Men.") So I had some knowledge, there was little or nothing written about spirituality for men, and I felt strongly about wanting to provide something for them. I went back to Saginaw and began listening and making notes on what men on the retreats were struggling with and looking for. Out of those notes and my previous experiences I wrote *A Man and His God: Contemporary Male Spirituality* (1988).

In 1995 the book went out of print. But every time I gave a retreat for men, I would get requests for copies of the book. So I decided to write another one. By this time I had collected a lot of new material, both from my experiences and from other authors who were writing about the spiritual needs of men. I had also worked out a new set of retreat conferences.

I have long been aware that I am not a very original thinker. My gift is the ability to "package" other people's ideas in a different way. So in this book the reader will find references to other contemporary authors from whom I have borrowed. The overall impression I hope to create is that interest in male spirituality is not a passing fad, but a growth in consciousness that is gaining momentum.

My intended audience is men who are searching for "something more" in life, who are not satisfied with the games and toys served up by the consumer culture. These men may or may not belong to a church or a religious denomination. No matter. The important thing is that they are seeking deeper spiritual meaning, a more personal relationship with God. The book reflects my Roman Catholic viewpoint, but I have tried to be inclusive of men who may be at a different point in their own spiritual journey. Besides my own theological tradition, I am strongly indebted to Professor Robert Hicks, Franciscan friar Richard Rohr, and the philosophy of Alcoholics Anonymous. Above all, I am grateful to the many men who have opened their souls and shared their spiritual journeys with me.

A final word about gender. Even though my previous book was written for men, I found that many women were not only buying it for the men in their lives but were reading it themselves. "Most of this stuff can be applied to anyone," they told me. I was pleased to hear that, and I hope the same is true for his new volume.

—*Martin Pable, Capuchin*

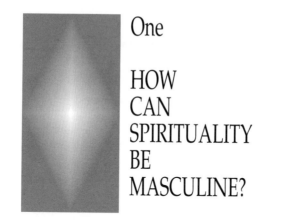

One

HOW CAN SPIRITUALITY BE MASCULINE?

In the years since my first book on male spirituality I have frequently been asked, "Is there really such a thing as 'masculine' (as opposed to 'feminine') spirituality?"

The question is a provocative one, and I have had to struggle with it myself. Often the best answer I have been able to come up with is, "I'm not sure." I know I did not write my first book with the intention of promoting the idea that there is a distinctive masculine spirituality. Rather, my purpose was to write a book on Christian spirituality for men.

Perhaps men and women do experience and live out their spirituality differently. That would be a fascinating research project. But the point I want to make is simply this: a lot of men in our society today do have a spiritual life, and many more have a desire for one. My evidence for this claim comes from a number of sources.

Naming the Pain

I find that men are becoming more open and vocal about their pain. This is especially true of "over-forty" males. Before that, guys are typically too busy "conquering" (in the workplace, the bedroom, the sports field, or wherever) to acknowledge that they are hurting in any way. To admit pain is neither cool nor macho. Robert Bly does a parody of a typical young male who is asked, "Hey, how's it goin'?" He responds, "I'm doin' fine, Jack. Eight women left me, and the last two beat me up—but I'm doin' fine!"

Nonetheless, when you put men together in a group and do a few things to create an atmosphere of trust, down come the defenses and out comes the pain. One of its sources is the pressure to achieve, to succeed, to move up the career ladder, to acquire more possessions and status symbols. What kind of a male are you if you don't run in the fast track? For a while the race can be exhilarating, but eventually the price gets increasingly high: fatigue, stress-related illnesses, neglect of intimate relationships. There is the nagging question: what's the point of it all?

Another source of pain for men is conflicting messages from the culture about masculinity. An interesting handout called "The Double Binds of Men" listed fourteen of them, but I'll just mention a few:

- ◆ The Feeling Bind: If a man lets his feelings show, he's judged to be weak, immature, effeminate; if he keeps emotions inside, he's deemed secretive, distant, and uninteresting.

- ◆ The Career-Ladder Bind: If a man works hard and keeps moving upward, he may be perceived as a workaholic and neglectful of his family; if he withdraws from the race in order to attend to self and family, he will be disvalued by his bosses and colleagues, and possibly resented by the family for not bringing in more goodies.

- ◆ The Child-Rearing Bind: If a man lets his wife do the primary or exclusive parenting, he will be seen as uncaring and uninvolved with his children; if he takes an active role in parenting, he may be resented for being a divisive influence.

- ◆ The Autonomy Bind: If a man tries to be independent

and self-reliant (in accord with the macho mystique), he may push others away and end up lonely and isolated; if he asks for help and appears to need others, he will be judged as unmasculine.

◆ The Health Bind: If a man pays attention to his body and takes good care of himself, he may be seen as a self-pampering hypochondriac; if he ignores symptoms and neglects good health habits, he sets himself up for major illness or emotional breakdown.

Sam Keen gives a vivid summary of the confusing and conflicting messages men receive from the contemporary culture:

> Ask most any man, "How does it feel to be a man these days? Do you feel manhood is honored, respected, celebrated?" Those who pause long enough to consider their gut feelings will likely tell you they feel blamed, demeaned, and attacked. But their reactions may be pretty vague. Many men feel as if they are involved in a night battle in a jungle against an unseen foe. Voices from the surrounding darkness shout hostile challenges: "Men are too aggressive. Too soft. Too insensitive. Too macho. Too power-mad. Too much like little boys. Too wimpy. Too violent. Too obsessed with sex. Too detached to care. Too busy. Too rational. Too lost to lead. Too dead to feel." Exactly what we are supposed to become is not clear (Keen 1991, 6).

Another source of pain for many men today is the criticism directed at them from some feminists. Men sometimes feel they are being blamed for everything wrong with the world: wars, inflation, crime and violence, domestic abuse, soaring divorce rates, illegitimacy, abandoned children, environmental pollution. What makes the pain even more acute is that many men have to admit that the criticism is valid to a great extent. It does not help them to feel good about themselves as males.

Yet another source of pain for men is what Richard Rohr

and others have called the "father-wound"; that is, many men today have never had a positive and life-affirming relationship with their fathers (or with uncles or other father figures). This has deprived them of healthy masculine energy and role models. I will reflect more on the father-wound in a later chapter.

Pain and Spirituality

A broad-based definition of spirituality could be: "whatever helps us make sense of our lives and gives them meaning." Some people's spirituality is a natural outgrowth of their good religious upbringing. For as long as they can remember, they have felt God close to them and tried to put Christ's teachings into practice. For many others, however, spirituality comes out of a need to find some way to deal with their pain. The prime example would be Alcoholics Anonymous and all of its spinoffs. The Twelve Steps clearly form a spiritual program, focused as they are on the need to rely on the power of God to help us manage our troubled lives. So a great number of men who acknowledge themselves to be addicted—whether to alcohol, drugs, work, sex, relationships— have found both sanity and spirituality through the Twelve Steps.

But AA and its derivatives are not the only places where men are discovering spirituality. Increasingly, they are coming together for retreats and conferences on issues of male identity, personal growth, dealing with stress, and finding spiritual meaning in life. Robert Bly conducts five-day retreats around the country. Richard Rohr draws capacity crowds for his Wilderness Retreats. My own retreat ministry to men has expanded considerably.

Besides retreats and conferences, men are gathering in small groups to share their concerns. For two years I met monthly with a group of twenty-five to thirty-five businessmen for a prayer breakfast and shared reflection on men's issues. The group continued with another leader after I left the area. A number of parishes have begun support or sharing groups for men. Men seem more willing to share their thoughts, feelings, and experiences in an all-male setting than in a mixed-sex group, where, for some reason I don't understand, men tend to withdraw and let women carry the discussion. There are exceptions, of course, but I have noticed the general trend often enough myself and have heard it confirmed by other observers.

It is not only personal pain or dissatisfaction with the roles and expectations that society has laid on men that is driving them to search for spirituality. More positively, it is their desire for wholeness. Men today often feel divided within themselves and isolated from the world around them. It is as if they are in grief over the loss of the Garden of Eden where man and woman were in harmony with one another, with nature, with the animals, and with God. Men long to feel that connectedness once again, and that is the beginning of a spiritual quest. Our word "religion" comes from the Latin *re-ligare* which means an ongoing binding process. So religion at its best is a set of beliefs and habits that binds us together, makes us whole, connects us to God, to one another, and to nature. Unfortunately, institutional religion sometimes gets enmeshed in laws and rituals that create divisions rather than wholeness. But even when men drop out of institutional religion, they usually do not lose their hunger for spirituality. The quest continues.

This fact was brought home to me very forcefully when I talked with Dr. Ian Harris of the University of Wisconsin-Milwaukee. He and I once teamed up to conduct a men's retreat during which he shared some of the research he was doing on men's spirituality. He had given questionnaires to and interviewed more than 600 men; some were practicing members of an organized religion, but many others were not. One of the questions he asked was: "On a scale of 1 to 10 (10 being the highest), how important is spirituality to your life as a whole?" When he analyzed the data, he was amazed to find that the average response was 8.7. To me, that statistic should forever lay to rest the common myth in our society that "real men" are not interested in religion or spiritual matters because "that's feminine stuff."

If we need any further evidence, all we have to do is take note of the Promise Keepers phenomenon. In 1990 a group of evangelical Christians noted that much pain in people's lives is created by men who make promises and then break them. So these men made a commitment to become promise *keepers* instead of breakers. At their first rally there were only seventy-five men. But each year the numbers grew. In 1993 the football stadium at Boulder, Colorado, was filled with 50,000 men of all Christian denominations (or no denomination), praying and singing aloud, listening to inspirational speakers ask them to commit themselves to regular prayer and Bible study, involvement with their families, support of their pastors, ethical and moral living, and fellowship with people of other faiths and races. The next year six such rallies around the country drew a total of 230,000 men. And in 1995, there were thirteen rallies with over 500,000 participants! I am not necessarily endorsing everything Promise Keepers stands for, but this spiritual movement of men cannot be ignored.

One more piece of data about men's quest for spirituality. Patrick Arnold, in *Wildmen, Warriors, and Kings,* invites us to look outside our own North American culture and into the temples, monasteries, and shrines of the world's religions. We will find, he says, "an astonishing variety of men fiercely plunging into the heart and center of their religions." In Japan, men study Zen under strict masters; in Thailand, a field of saffron-clothed monks sit reverently before the Buddha; in India, an ocean of men make pilgrimage to Benares; in Muslim countries, men drop to their knees in prayer five times a day; in Jerusalem, Jewish men pray devoutly at the Western Wall; in South Dakota, Lakota Sioux males pray and purify themselves in sweat lodges; in France, the ecumenical brothers of Taize chant their praises to God and by their simple life of prayer and mutual love draw groups of young pilgrims from all over the world. By such a mental journey, Arnold says, "one joins in the world-wide symphony of a billion male voices praising God, repenting of sins, crying for visions, and seeking help along life's painful road. It has been going on for ten thousand years" (Arnold 1991, 72).

What Is Spirituality?

Earlier I defined spirituality broadly as "whatever helps us make sense of our lives and gives them meaning." This could include such diverse endeavors as Twelve-Step programs, New Age beliefs, and humanistic psychology. But now I want to sharpen our focus. I am, after all, a Christian. I believe in a transcendent God as well as in the God-man, Jesus Christ. I suspect that most of my readers share these basic beliefs. Somehow our spirituality must connect us with these realities. So, we can redefine spirituality as "the ongoing endeavor to grow in our relationship with God."

Let's take a closer look at that definition. First of all, spirituality is an *endeavor*. It is not simply a set of concepts or beliefs to keep in our head. It is both a vision of life and a way of living in accord with that vision. In other words, it is choice and it is action-oriented; spirituality ought to give direction not only to our thinking, but also to our decision-making. Secondly, it is an *ongoing* endeavor. That is, spirituality is not something we eventually finish, like a job or a project. We attend to it, nurture it, refine it till the day we die. Like the biblical notion of conversion, spirituality is dynamic and never-ending. And third, its goal is growth in our relationship with God. This assumes that we already have a relationship with God; the task is to develop and deepen it, much like any other relationship. To do so requires spiritual discipline, such as Scripture reading and personal prayer (I will have more to say about this in the final chapter).

For now, however, I want to focus on something more immediate. One of the obstacles to spiritual growth that I often find in my work with men is that many men are not convinced that they have a personal relationship with God. At least, they don't think in those terms. Rather, they think of spirituality exclusively in terms of practices such as praying, attending Mass, going to confession, helping their neighbor. None of this is wrong, of course, but it does not get to the heart of spirituality. After all, I might succeed in doing all of the above for the wrong reasons: to avoid going to hell, to feel good about myself, to impress my neighbors, to keep my wife from nagging. To use an analogy, it would be like a golfer concentrating on keeping his head down, bending his right knee, cocking his wrists, following through—but forgetting that the object of the game is to hit the ball onto the green and into the cup.

A great truth is that spirituality, in the Christian tradition, begins with God, not with self. *Psychologically,* however, it begins with us, in the sense that at some point we sense our incompleteness, our loneliness, our profound limitations, our disillusion with all that merely glitters and seduces, our longing for something or someone that can truly fill us. Consciously or unconsciously, we are searching for God.

But the blessed message, the good news of the Scriptures, is that God is in search of us. When Adam and Eve hid in the Garden of Eden, God came looking for them. "Where are you?" God asks; as if to say, "I miss you." The gentle question unmasks the sin and deceit of the couple, but it also begins the healing. God is saying, "Can we talk? Can we start over again?" This dynamic occurs over and over in the Scriptures, from the story of the Fall to Jesus' parable of the lost sheep, in which the shepherd (image of God) goes out in search of the one who strayed. It also appears in the scene where Jesus is saying, "Behold, I stand at the door and knock. If anyone hears my voice and opens the door, I will enter his house and dine with him, and he with me" (Rv 3:20). The door is a symbol of the human heart. Notice again who takes the initiative. It is Christ who comes knocking and calling to us. But he will never force his way into our lives. We must open the door of our heart to him, and that can only be done from the inside— that is, from our own free will. But if we make that choice, Jesus says, he will come in and share a meal with us. To share a meal in the Middle East is always a sign of special friend-ship. Once again, we are back to the very essence of spiritual-ity: a personal relationship.

So, first of all, God is always reaching out to us, inviting us. That is the first movement of spirituality. The second movement is up to us: We can choose either to ignore the invi-tation or to respond by committing ourselves to a personal relationship with God (or with Jesus Christ, if we find it easi-er to relate to him; it really doesn't matter, because one Divine Person will eventually draw us into relationship with all three Persons of the Trinity).

When I say we can choose to ignore God's invitation, I'm not necessarily implying that this is a conscious decision. Most of the time, I think, we are simply too distracted or preoccupied to recognize that we are being addressed by God. I once heard Anthony De Mello say that our society keeps giving us "drugs" that dull our spiritual awareness: consumer products; forms of entertainment; all-absorbing work; the need to look good, to be accepted, to feel powerful. With our senses and imagination tuned to all this, it is difficult indeed to hear the call of God in the depths of our souls.

"Waking Up"

But many of us do manage to "wake up." Some men have been conscientious and faithful Christians all their lives. They have formed the habit of tuning in to God by way of prayer, Bible reading, and participation in Mass and the other sacraments. Their spirituality has grown by evolution and regular nurturance. Other men may have coasted along for years on the externals of religious practice, but without the sense of personal relationship with God. Then one day they read a book, hear a sermon, attend a Bible class, make a retreat, and they are struck with an awesome truth: the love of God, the miracles in the gospels, the real presence of Christ in the eucharist are not just words. They are profound truths with life-changing power.

Still others have had to go through a rather rude awakening: alcoholics who have hit bottom; men jilted by lovers
who confronted them on their character defects; men whose
careers have been shattered by company downsizing and
restructuring; men who have made work their god and then
discovered it was costing them their soul; men who have been
jolted by a stroke or a heart attack; men who have pursued the
American dream and found themselves disillusioned. The
common thread here is the realization—gradual or sudden—
that there has to be more. And then they start paying attention
to their inner world, that quiet place in the soul where they
find God waiting.

Personal Commitment

Whatever form the awakening takes, the next movement
of spirituality is personal commitment. We find ourselves saying, though maybe not in so many words, "Lord Jesus, whatever it means, I want to surrender myself to you. I don't want
to live just for myself. I want you to be at the center of my life.
I accept your gift of friendship, and I ask you to help me live
as you want me to live."

I fear that the Catholic church has not sufficiently empha-
sized this dynamic of personal commitment. Perhaps we have
been preoccupied with revising the liturgy, changing church
organization, and motivating people to get involved in social
justice. These are all necessary, but we have to take care that we
do not lose our center. Bishop Raymond Lucker of New Ulm,
Minnesota, once noted that too many Catholics have been
taught rules and doctrines but not the joy of having a personal
relationship with Jesus Christ.

We all know men who are hard-working, responsible,
good family men. They attend Sunday Mass regularly and
may even go to confession once or twice a year. But there is
no heart, no enthusiasm in their religion. It is like a separate
compartment that never spills over into the other compartments of their lives. They are not involved in their parish,

apart from helping to set up booths at the annual festival. Knowledge of their religion remains at the elementary or high school level. They willingly attend courses and workshops to improve themselves on their jobs, but they never think of doing something similar for their Christianity. These men belong to the vast army of "Sunday Catholics," dutifully plodding along on the road to salvation.

This is why a lot of men are saying, "There's got to be more." And they're right. Spirituality ought to be energizing and life-enhancing, not a drag. Jesus said, "I came so that they might have life and have it more abundantly" (Jn 10:10). Men have confided in me some of the wonderful things that began to happen to them when they opened themselves to a personal relationship with God. They came to know God's presence and love in a new way, a personal way: "I guess I knew a lot *about* God," they say, "but now I know *God*." They experience Jesus Christ as their friend, walking with them, guiding them in their decisions, strengthening them in times of stress. They find it easy to talk to him in prayer. The words of Scripture take on new and personal meaning. Instead of worrying so much about their problems, they feel a deep peace and have confidence in the Lord's power to help them. Even their limitations and mistakes don't seem so horrendous any more, because they feel loved and accepted in the core of their being.

Connecting Spirituality with Life

Empowered by the presence of Christ and the gifts of the Holy Spirit, a man is now ready for the fourth movement of spirituality: forming a vision and a lifestyle in line with his commitment. Instead of keeping separate compartments, he begins to make connections—first in his mind, then in his choices. He begins to ask new questions: How does God view this issue? What is the Lord's plan for sexuality? How does my job fit into God's larger purposes for me and for the world? How does God view my marriage, my children, my style of parenting? What does Christ teach about human relations and dealing with difficult people?

Instead of relying on his own judgments and insights, the man seeks guidance through prayer, reading the Bible and other spiritual sources, and seeking the counsel of other faith-filled people. As he grows in vision, he also comes to see that his actions and choices need to be brought into line. Here is where the going can get tough, because he may reach the conclusion that he has to make some changes in his lifestyle if he is going to be faithful to the newfound vision. As one man told me, "Spirituality was fun till I realized it meant giving God the right to ask some things of me!"

Let's be very clear about this. Spirituality is not meant to be fun and games. It is discipline, and it is tough.

This is the reason that in *A Man and His God* I stressed the importance of the traditional spiritual disciplines, especially prayer and Bible reading. Then I tried to make connections between spirituality and some of the key areas of a man's life: self-image, work and leisure, the quest for love, marriage and family, dealing with life's problems.

A Different Approach

Here I want to use a different approach, one inspired by Robert Hicks, a Protestant minister, in *The Masculine Journey*. Hicks describes being a guest on a talk show. Suddenly the host turned and asked him, "So, what is a man?" Hicks found himself talking in circles, backpedaling, quoting other writers, embarrassed that he couldn't give a coherent answer. Pondering this question later he was able to retrieve from his memory six Hebrew words for man found in the Hebrew Scriptures. He had also been reading Daniel Levinson's *The Seasons of a Man's Life*, and he liked the idea that manhood is experienced differently at different times in the life cycle. With those two insights, Hicks worked out the notion of "the masculine journey," using the six Hebrew words to describe six different moments or stages of a man's spiritual development.

At this point let us look briefly at the six Hebrew words and the corresponding life stages as presented by Robert Hicks:

'Adam ("created"): We are not derived from ourselves; we receive our existence from the creative power of God. Herein lies our profound dignity as humans: we are made in the image of God. But *'adam* also signifies our fragility and mortality; we are not in total control of our lives or our world.

Zakar ("phallic"): While *'adam* can refer to either the male or the female of the human species, *zakar* speaks of the sexual differentiation of the male. He possesses a phallus, a source of positive sexual energy, but one that requires regulation in accord with the divine plan.

Gibbor ("warrior"): This aspect of manhood has to do with strength, combat, and competition. This energy needs to be directed toward the right kind of goals or it will become a destructive force in the life of the individual as well as of society.

Enosh ("wounded"): Sooner or later the warrior is hurt. Life has a thousand ways of wounding the male. How he deals with the hurt will have profound effects on his spiritual development.

'Ish ("ruler"): This is the man of maturity. The man has learned to rule his own spirit, and he is able to exercise authority for the good of the community—family, business, civic, and ecclesial. At the same time, he is able to share power and authority without feeling threatened in his manhood.

Zaken ("gray-haired"): The man is full of years and experience, still making contributions to his community and passing on a spiritual legacy to family and society.

I hope to make use of Hicks's basic categories in conjunction with my own experience and my Catholic spiritual tradition. I will modify or depart from Hicks's insights at times; and I will make connections of my own, particularly with the gospels and other writings from the Christian Scriptures. I will also try to highlight both the creative possibilities and the stressful challenges that are present at each stage of the journey.

Like Hicks, I do not see these stages as rigidly chronological. As men, he says, "we live at many points on the map at the same time. In this sense the stopping places are more logical than chronological" (Hicks 1993, 28). Nor do we move through each stage, never to return. Our journey is much more circular. We never cease being created, sexual beings; we have to summon our warrior energy and courage repeatedly during life; we are wounded again and again; we use our ruling power well at some times and badly at others; age alone is not a reliable indicator of wisdom. Still, I find the categories useful, because they represent tasks, skills, and challenges that confront us at various stages of life's journey. They engage our very soul as they bring us face to face with life's ultimate questions.

That's the "stuff" of spirituality.

Two

MAN: CREATED IN GOD'S IMAGE

'*Adam* is the first Hebrew word for "man" in the Bible. The word is applied to both males and females. As such it describes our basic common humanity. The Bible makes it clear that we did not create ourselves or simply evolve by chance from lower life forms. The operative words here are "by chance," for it is not contrary to our faith to believe that humans did indeed evolve from lower species. What we do believe is that the process was wondrously guided by the creative plan of God, and that humans are in some way a special creation of God.

The Bible pictures God as forming '*adam* out of the clay or mud of the earth (*adama* in Hebrew). The play on words reveals the "earthy" nature of '*adam*. He is definitely not God, though the devil will later try to deceive '*adam* into thinking he is God's equal. Interestingly, one of the affirmations of recovering alcoholics is, "We have to learn to stop playing God." There are only two things AA says about God: first, there is one; and second, it's not *you*.

But the clearest message of this first chapter of the Bible is the dignity of '*adam*: "God created man in his image; in the divine image he created him; male and female he created them. God blessed them. . . (Gn 1:27-28).

Our Experience of Shame

We need to dwell on this verse from Genesis for a while, because so many people in our society do not feel themselves "blessed" with God-given dignity. Instead, they suffer from low self-esteem. A priest who gives retreats for youth asks the teens to make a double list: first, their flaws and negative qualities; and second, their good points. Inevitably, he says, they come up with a lengthy list of negatives and only one or two positives. No doubt this is a phase that most adolescents go through; the tragedy is that a lot of adults never move beyond it. Here is a remarkable irony: Americans as a society are healthy, educated, and affluent, yet we suffer, as James Dobson says, from "an epidemic of inferiority."

What is going on here? John Bradshaw, in his writings and television programs, uses the powerful word *shame* to describe the core feeling of many people. I was struck by the vivid description of shame given by Lewis Smedes:

> The feeling of shame is about our very *selves*—not about some bad thing we did or said, but about what we *are*. It tells us that we *are* unworthy. Totally. It is not as if a few seams in the garment of our selves need stitching; the whole fabric is frayed. We feel that we *are* unacceptable. And to feel that is a life-wearying heaviness. Shame-burdened people are the sort whom Jesus had in mind when he invited the "weary and heavy laden" to trade their heaviness for his lightness (Smedes 1993, 6).

Note that this feeling of shame is not the same as guilt. The emotional tone may be quite similar, but there are sharp differences. For one thing, guilt arises from some action or omission on our part, something we did or failed to do. But shame arises from our perception of who we *are*, our very core. Instead of saying, "I sinned, I failed, I made a mistake," we say, "I *am* my sin, I am a failure, I am a mistake." Talk about a heavy burden!

Second, guilt can be a healthy emotion, moving us to repentance, apology, conversion, self-correction. The negative feeling lifts with time, and we move on. Shame, however, is relentless. No matter how often we confess or apologize, we still feel ashamed. In fact, even our obvious successes or the affirmations of others don't make a dent in the feeling that we will never be good enough.

Where do these feelings of shame come from? Psychologists suggest we look first of all to our family of origin. Indeed, parents and other family members can find numerous ways of shaming us, sometimes without intending to do so. They let us know that they are disappointed with us: we are the wrong sex, have the wrong color eyes or hair, are not intelligent enough, not athletic enough, not competitive enough, not . . . not. . . .

Priest-psychiatrist Vincent Dwyer tells a poignant story about growing up in a New England family. His father made a living as a clam-digger. For some reason, probably out of his own feelings of low status, he kept telling young Vincent: "You're a dummy! You'll never amount to anything more than a clam-digger's son." So Vincent made up his mind to prove his father wrong. He studied hard in high school, got into college, and went on to get an M.D. When he graduated from medical school, his father was there. After the ceremony, he went up to Vincent and said, with real warmth, "Son, I want you to know how proud I am of you!"

Vincent looked at him and said, "Dad, that's the first time I ever heard you say that. All my life you cut me down and told me how dumb I was."

"What? You mean all those years I was working and providing for you, you didn't think I loved you?"

"No, Dad, I didn't."

"Boy, you really are a dummy!"

We can speculate here that Vincent's father, in his own clumsy way, was probably trying "to keep the boy from getting a big head." Fortunately, Vincent did not internalize the negative messages; instead, he turned them into positive energy to prove his father wrong. Most youngsters, however, are not able to do this. They either "swallow" the shame messages and grow to adulthood with a chronic sense of inferiority, or they rebel and turn their anger against authority figures.

Another major source of shame is the wider culture. What does the secular world hold up as the "ideal male"? He is college-educated, has the perfect body of an athlete, is an irresistible sex partner, is tough and competitive on the job but smart enough to stay out of trouble and not make waves, owns a nice home and a classy car, is sophisticated in the ways of the world and knows just what to wear on all occasions. Who can live up to that? Failure to achieve this cultural ideal is all too easy, indeed inevitable.

Healing for Our Shame

I am not saying that all men come out of shame-driven families or have internalized the "you're not good enough" messages. Many have been able to find some remedy. A good number of people today find help in the experience of psychotherapy. A good therapist can help them name their feelings of shame and inadequacy and trace their sources. Hopefully, they can then move on to forgive those who have shamed them and begin to build a positive sense of self-worth based on a realistic reappraisal of themselves and their capabilities.

Educators and school counselors are also working to improve children's self-esteem. This is certainly a laudable goal. But recently a number of observers, myself included, have expressed some reservations about the "self-esteem movement." For one thing, it can foster a self-centered, demanding, arrogant attitude. We have all met children and teens who act as though their rights are the only ones that matter. Ann Landers tells about the nine-year-old who announced, "I'm running away tomorrow; who's going to drive me?" Moreover, warnings about the bad effects of guilt and shame can make adults hesitant to scold or even to correct a child for inappropriate behavior. So the line between right and wrong becomes more and more blurred. Even healthy guilt has to be exorcised. How else can we explain the cruel and criminal actions of youth whose only response, when they are caught, is to snicker and act "cool"? No sign of remorse. No admission of wrongdoing.

Once again, browsing through a bookstore can reveal a great deal about the mindset of our culture. If aliens from another planet looked over the shelves of self-help books, they would come away with the impression that ours is the most self-absorbed culture in the universe. The purpose of such books is to help people with poor self-esteem to start valuing themselves more. Who can argue with that? But so often, it seems to me, this positive outcome appears to be obtained only at the expense of diminishing or ignoring others. I can't imagine how this can produce any genuine or lasting healing for our shame.

So, I have to ask, what is the ultimate philosophical basis for claiming value as a person? "You are good!" the books and therapists say. "You are worthwhile." "You are lovable." "You deserve to be happy." I agree. But what is it that enables them to make those statements, and what enables others to believe them? By what authority are they speaking? In their own name? In the name of Carl Jung? Karen Horney? Abraham Maslow? Carl Rogers? All of the above?

I had the same uneasy feeling when I read the 1970s bestseller *I'm OK, You're OK*. It sounded so right, and it was so much in harmony with my beliefs as a Christian. But the author could give no real grounding for the claim of "OKness" except that it "worked." That is, if I believe that I am OK (a worthwhile person) and that others are also OK, I will be happier inside and will treat others better than if I believe otherwise. So we're really talking about an act of faith—in myself or in my therapist.

Then I read an article by theologian-psychologist Thomas Oden entitled "Who Says You're OK?" He showed very convincingly that the belief in my own and others' goodness is illusory unless it is grounded is some reality larger and deeper than any human word. The good news of the Scriptures, Oden says, is that there is indeed an ultimate, transcendent Word in the universe—nothing less than the Word of God—that declares us OK, worthwhile and lovable, that blesses us and pronounces us good (Gn 1:28,31).

Let's look at the testimony of Scripture for this healing and liberating Word:

◆ In the prophet Isaiah we read: "But now, thus says the Lord, who created you, O Jacob, and formed you, O Israel: Fear not, for I have redeemed you; I have called you by name: you are mine. . . . Because you are precious in my eyes and glorious, and because I love you. . . . Fear not, for I am with you" (Is 43:1,4-5).

◆ Jesus tells his disciples (and us): "Are not two sparrows sold for a small coin? Yet not one of them falls to the ground without your Father's knowledge. Even all the hairs of your head are counted. So do not be afraid; you are worth more than many sparrows. (Mt 10:29-31). Notice that Jesus says we can be free of both shame and fear because God holds us in such high regard. Fr. John Shea said that one of our deepest fears is that we are forgettable. But Jesus assures us that we will not be forgotten by God, who does not forget even the lowly sparrows.

◆ Not only that, but St. Paul says that God chose us and blessed us in Christ even before the foundation of the world (Eph 1:3-4).

◆ The Letter of Peter reminds us that we are "a chosen race, royal priesthood, a holy nation, a people of his own (1 Pt 2:9). That's more appealing and encouraging than being told, "You're OK!" And because God has graced us with such dignity, Peter says, "Cast all your cares on him, because he cares for you" (1 Pt 5:7).

I think it's also important to note that our God-given dignity is prior to, and independent of, any of our accomplishments. That seems especially significant for us males, since we are prone to measure ourselves by our achievements. That's why I think infant baptism is such a counter-cultural practice. It's a great way to challenge society's whole system of valuing people on the basis of performance. Here is this tiny infant who has absolutely no accomplishments to its credit, yet the family, the church, and even God are all telling it how blessed and welcome it is. "Little baby," they say, "as time goes on we will expect more of you; there will be tasks to perform and roles to be filled. But right now we commit ourselves to giving you one great positive message: You are precious, you are holy, just because you are a child of God and one of our human family."

A Man Flawed and Divided

So the Scriptures make it clear that *'adam* is created with profound dignity, because he is made in the image of God. Unlike God, however, he is not perfect. There is some deep and radical flaw in his nature. Robert Hicks describes it as "savagery"—the whole set of tendencies to self-glorification, greed, domination, ambition, addiction, violence, and so on. "Though we are made in the image of God," Hicks says, "possessing great capabilities for good, we are also free to pursue unholy courses."

I don't especially like the image of savagery to name this aspect of *'adam*, but we all know what Hicks is saying. Who among us has not been embarrassed, even appalled, by some word or behavior that has burst out of us from we know not where? We take a nasty verbal swipe at our wife or child; we pad our expense account; we tell a bald lie to cover up a mistake. What St. Paul wrote about himself sounds remarkably appropriate: "What I do, I do not understand…for I do not do the good I want, but I do the evil I do not want"(Rom 7:15,19). The traditional name for this inner defect is *original sin*. There is some basic flaw in our nature that divides us; we know we are called to image the goodness and holiness of God, but there is always that drive to self-interest and self-indulgence instead.

Some time ago I came across *The Spirituality of Imperfection* by Ernest Kurtz and Katherine Ketcham. The title intrigued me because we are used to thinking about spirituality as striving for perfection. The authors quote Fay Vincent, former commissioner of baseball, as saying that "baseball teaches us how to deal with failure." Even a good batter, he reminds us, fails to get a hit two out of three times. "I also find it fascinating," he says, "that baseball considers errors to be part of the game, part of its rigorous truth."

The authors go on to say that the "rigorous truth" about human life is that we are all flawed. That is part of being *'adam*. As Ralph Waldo Emerson once said, "There is a crack in everything God made." The most beautiful flowers bloom only for a short time. Mighty trees eventually decay. Even the majestic mountains get worn down. Why should we expect *'adam* to be perfect?

Kurtz and Ketcham also tell a story about a preacher who asked a group of children, "If all the good people in the world were colored green, and all the bad people colored red—what color would you be?" A little girl replied, "Preacher, I reckon I'd be streaked!"

Perfect answer. We are all a mixture: light/dark; beauty/ugliness; nobility/nastiness. The trouble is, many males don't want to face this "rigorous truth." We seem unable to accept the simple fact that we are human and have weaknesses. We have accepted too readily the culture's irrational demands that to be a man means to be strong, to be successful, to be in control. There is little or no room for human error, for mistakes, for sins. Is it any wonder that so many men carry around burdens of shame and self-doubt or drive themselves to measure up to an impossible ideal? If only they could accept themselves as *'adam*—earthy, flawed, limited, yet carrying within themselves the dignity and spark of divinity.

Another "rigorous truth" that *'adam* is called to embrace

is the fact of his mortality. Facing this reality does not come easily, particularly in contemporary American society. In 1975 psychiatrist Ernest Becker wrote *The Denial of Death,* in which he showed how, both individually and collectively, we spend much psychic energy to protect ourselves from the fear of death. Some time ago there was a segment on television showing how, for an astronomical fee, a person can have his or her dead body frozen and preserved in the hope that someday science will discover an elixir that will "cure" everything and enable the person to be revived and live forever.

The Bible allows us no such illusion. *'Adam* is mortal by his very nature. His existence is neither self-created, nor is it self-sustained. The fact, time, and circumstances of his death are totally outside his control. Psalm 49 is a reflection on the foolishness of thinking that acquiring riches can provide protection from death:

Yet in no way can a man (*'adam*) redeem himself,
　　or pay his own ransom to God. . . .
For he can see that wise men die,
　　and likewise the senseless and the stupid pass
　　　　away,
　　leaving to others their wealth. . . .
Thus man, for all his splendor, does not abide;
　　he resembles the beasts that perish (Ps 49:8,11,13).

As Hicks notes, males are particularly inclined to deny their mortality: "We think we will live forever; we won't have heart attacks, lose our capabilities, our health, or our minds. But sooner or later . . . we must face the startling revelation that life must be lived within the limits of breath and death" (Hicks 1993, 38).

I have observed the same tendency to deny mortality myself. So many men, it seems to me, are reluctant to visit sick people. They ignore physical symptoms and avoid doctors "like the plague," to use an inept metaphor. Why? Probably because these are all reminders of mortality. "Sometimes," Garrison Keillor once said, "you have to look reality right in the eye—and deny it!" I truly believe, though, that once we embrace the fact of our mortality, we become free to live fully and deeply "within the limits of breath and death."

Care for Our Health

One of my current jobs is to direct a wellness program for our Capuchin friars. I have had to do a lot of reading and talking to health professionals about preventive health maintenance. While good health is partly a gift of God from our parents' genes, it is also the fruit of some basic lifestyle habits over which we have a high degree of control: not smoking; adequate sleep; good nutrition; regular exercise; regular health checkups; reduction of stress; and a balanced life. I will discuss the last two more fully in a later chapter, but let me say a brief word about the other ingredients of preventive health:

Not smoking: The scientific evidence is overwhelming that smoking is a high-risk factor in diseases of the heart as well as in many forms of cancer. I have a great deal of compassion for men who are addicted to smoking. It can be a very difficult habit to break, but my hope is that they will make the effort and seek help if needed.

Adequate sleep: The need for sleep varies greatly among humans, but many adults require about seven hours a night. We each need to find our own optimal time. Unfortunately, many men deprive themselves of needed sleep in order to keep up the pace of work they have set for themselves or allowed others to demand of them.

Nutrition: Eating is surely one of life's great pleasures. But more and more people today are learning how to "eat smart." This means, basically, cutting back on red meat, dairy products, candy and pastries, and most processed foods; increasing the intake of fruits, vegetables, and whole grains; and substituting nonfat or low-fat products for their high-fat counterparts wherever possible. Excess weight also increases the risks of heart disease and high blood pressure. Men who have problems controlling their weight can get help from a credible weight-loss program, from their physician, or from a registered dietitian.

Exercise: Evidence continues to mount that regular, moderate, aerobic (large-muscle) exercise is a major factor in maintaining good health. This means, for example, twenty minutes on an exercise bike or thirty minutes of walking at a moderate pace. Those who can do this daily, or even three or four times a week, will be doing a great favor for their heart, lungs, circulatory system, and digestive system. And all studies have shown that it is never too late to begin.

Regular physical checkups: All the literature I've read stresses the value of prevention-oriented health screening. For men over fifty, most health-care professionals recommend a good physical exam once a year. Modern methods have made these checkups less of an ordeal than they used to be. The basics include a blood pressure reading; check of heart and lungs; one blood sample to check for cholesterol, blood sugar, and prostate cancer; and a non-invasive test called hemoccult for colon/rectal cancer.

I'm dwelling a bit on preventive health maintenance because I see a clear link between care for our health and spirituality. Our body, after all, is the servant of our spirit. If we neglect or abuse our body, we are diminishing its capacity to fulfill the tasks we have been given by God. We are not being good stewards of God's gifts. We all know what happens when we ignore symptoms of malfunctioning in our cars or don't keep up the normal maintenance schedule. Eventually we get stuck with a major overhaul and a huge bill. How much more true when it's a matter of caring for our own body.

Created for Relationship

One final aspect of 'adam is that he is created for relationship. He is not to live in isolation but in harmony with other humans, with his environment, and with God. The Bible teaches this truth in a very simple and touching way when it pictures God saying, "It is not good for 'adam to be alone. I will make a suitable partner for him" (Gn 2:18). Then God proceeds to create woman, brings her to *'adam*, and blesses their union of body and spirit (Gn 2:22-23). That is the Bible's way of teaching that human love, companionship, sex, marriage, and children are all God-given.

Marriage and family are not the only ties that bind us to one another as humans, of course. The Scriptures are abundantly clear that *'adam* is called to care for all others of the species. God rebukes Cain when he tries to deny responsibility for his brother (Gn 4:9). The prophets were forever confronting Israel's leaders for their neglect and downright oppression of the poor and marginal people of the land. Jesus told the story of the Good Samaritan when some of his listeners wanted to confine their caring outreach only to those of "our kind." And he asked his disciples not to limit their love to those who love them in return; but to bless and pray even for those who mistreat them (Lk 6:27-35).

But *'adam's* care extends even to the nonhuman creation. Man and woman together are formed in the image of God (Gn 1:27) and therefore are God's representatives on earth. He placed them "in the garden of Eden, to cultivate and care for it" (Gn 2:15). So *'adam* is to continue God's work of creation and bring it to greater perfection. Another term for *'adam's* role is environmental stewardship. When the Bible says that God gave *'adam* "dominion" over the rest of creation (Gn 1:28), it does not mean license to exploit the earth's natural resources, thereby causing the extinction of so many species of trees, plants, and animals. Rather, God is asking *'adam* to make wise use of the resources, to practice conservation, to maintain the ecological balance of the planet, and to keep the earth healthy and life-giving for his children, grandchildren, and all future generations.

Pope John Paul II drew upon these biblical truths to develop a profound theology of human work in his encyclical *Laborem Exercens*. Basically, he said that God has chosen to make us partners in the ongoing mystery of creation. As I wrote earlier:

Think of the implications of this. When human beings

discover cures for disease, when they find healing therapies for mental and emotional distress, when they produce better and safer modes of transportation, when they improve agricultural methods, when they build cleaner and healthier cities, when they find better ways of communicating and processing information, when they equip all citizens with the knowledge and skills they need for meaningful employment—in these and thousands of other ways they are engaging in tasks that are truly sacred, because they are fulfilling the plan of God (Pable 1988, 62-63).

Finally, it is the very nature of 'adam to be in relationship with God. Tragically, too many men spend too much of their lives attempting to run away from this relationship. Sometimes it is because they are afraid of what God may ask of them. Sometimes it is because the God they have been taught or shown is a caricature, a harsh, demanding, killjoy figure. Sometimes they have been led to believe that religion is for women or for wimpy, dependent men. Sometimes their own pride, arrogance, or sinful attachments keep them from letting God into their life.

I do not believe that men will ever be whole unless and until they find their proper relationship with God. With Robert Hicks, I believe that all men are "Christ-haunted." Once they understand Christianity as a personal relationship with Christ and are able to see the healthy masculinity of Christ, they find healing.

Without accepting the creaturely realities of being made by and for our heavenly Father, we cannot be the men we should be. This is the beginning point, the first stop on the male journey. Without beginning here we won't develop any further. Without this relationship, we won't grow up as men and become the men we were made to be (Hicks 1993, 35).

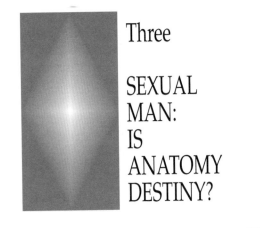

Three

SEXUAL MAN: IS ANATOMY DESTINY?

The Hebrew word *'adam* embodies the most fundamental truth about what it means to be a man. It tells us that we are created by God, not self-made; that we are earthy, limited, fragile, mortal, and yet bear a God-given dignity and an immortal spirit; and that we are not made to be alone, that we are created for relationship with one another, with the rest of nature, and with God. *'Adam* is indeed a word rich with layers of meaning.

When we come to the second Hebrew word for man, it is much more focused. The word is *zakar,* and it refers directly to the male sexual organ, the phallus. The root meaning of the word is "to be sharp or pointed," while the corresponding word for woman is *neqevah,* meaning "bored through or pierced." *Zakar* is used eighty-two times in the Hebrew Scriptures to refer to man in contrast to woman. "In other words," Robert Hicks says, "the Scriptures root male identity and sexuality firmly in anatomy, rather than in psychology or sociology" (Hicks 1993, 48). The Bible's *zakar* says, "I am a male, whether I feel like it or not, or whether I ever do anything considered masculine by the culture in which I am living." This is not to say that a man is totally defined by his phallus; that is a skewed notion that too many males in our society have been shaped to believe. But it is to say that sexual anatomy is a primary determinant of one's identity and cannot be divorced from spirituality.

Zakar as Symbol of Dedication to God

For the Hebrew male, the phallus was not just the organ of sexual activity; it had spiritual significance, for it was the sign of his dedication to God. This covenant symbolism is stated clearly in Genesis:

> When Abram was ninety-nine years old, the Lord appeared to him and said: "I am God the Almighty. Walk in my presence and be blameless. Between you and me I will establish my covenant, and I will multiply you exceedingly. . . . On your part, you and your descendants must keep my covenant throughout the ages. This is my covenant with you and your descendants after you that you must keep: every male among you shall be circumcised. Circumcise the flesh of your foreskin, and that shall be the mark of the covenant between you and me" (Gn 17:1-2,9-11).

Note how earthy and vivid the mark of covenant is. As Hicks says, "it is the male organ that is singled out as the unique site for the first wound and bloodletting a man will face" (Hicks 1993, 52). But circumcision is not a ritual for enduring pain; it is a religious rite, a wound that symbolically joins the male child to God from the first days of his life. Was there a similar ritual for girls? Yes, there was. When a girl was born, the parents would lift her high and offer a prayer of consecration; she too was a child of God and a participant in the covenant with her people.

For the male, however, circumcision was a visible, unmistakable reminder of who he was: a child/man of God. His sexuality had spiritual significance. Moreover, circumcision gave the male tribal and ethnic identity: he was a Hebrew. This became increasingly important as Jews began to mingle and interact with Gentiles. The circumcised Jew had to remember that he was different, that he belonged to a unique community, dedicated to a unique and transcendent God.

In the New Covenant, circumcision was abolished—and for good reasons. Christians came to realize that Jesus Christ broke down the barriers between Jews and Gentiles, between males and females, between ethnic and racial groups. All people are now called to live in communion with God and with one another. All are offered the gift of healing, salvation, and eternal life. So circumcision was replaced by baptism, a ritual that powerfully symbolizes death to all sin and self-seeking, and to all barriers that would divide one race, sex, or class from another. At the same time, it symbolizes resurrection to a new life of love in accord with the new commandment of Jesus: "Love one another as I love you" (Jn 15:12).

This law of love was a great leap forward in spiritual consciousness. Yet I think we need to acknowledge that something was lost in abandoning ritual circumcision: the connection between sexuality and spirituality. Christianity has been struggling to heal that split ever since. Eugene Monick observes: "People are uneasy with the correlation of sexuality and religion. . . . The church elevates religion, devaluing sexuality. Psychiatry does the opposite—elevating sexuality and devaluing religion. The union of sexuality and religion is like an electrical connection. Wrong joining leads to disaster. No joining produces no energy. Proper joining holds promise" (Hicks 1993, 54).

Wouldn't it be marvelous if men could stop: a) being ashamed of their phallus; and b) making a god out of it? If they could rediscover the sacred connection between the phallus and their covenant relationship with God? Perhaps then they could take delight in their sexual power *and* recognize the need for its regulation, in harmony with the divine plan. In fact, if we understand the sacrament of baptism deeply enough, it is clear that it is our total person, not just the phallus, that is joined to God in the ritual action. This truth is highlighted especially when baptism is done by total immersion. The symbolism is unmistakable; *all* of our body and its functions have sacred significance. There are profound implications here for the way we care for our body, the way we treat one another, and the way we make love. The dignity of the human body is also the basis for the church's teachings on reverence for life as well as on the proper use of sexuality.

Rites of Initiation

From a developmental standpoint, *zakar* takes on heightened significance during adolescence. This is when the young man's sexuality becomes a conscious preoccupation. Recently a number of writers on men's issues have noted a conspicuous absence in our culture of any meaningful rites of passage for adolescents. There are no socially agreed-upon rituals or processes to help adolescents deal constructively with their newly awakened sexuality or, for that matter, other social-emotional issues that press upon them. Indeed, given the diversity of racial, cultural and religious groups in this nation, it would be difficult to agree upon forms such initiation processes ought to take. So it is left up to the parents or, in many cases, to the adolescents themselves to navigate through these confusing waters.

If we look beyond our own culture, however, we observe some interesting contrasts. Richard Rohr, in one of his taped retreats for men, notes that primal cultures all have initiation rites for young males, and that these all involve some kind of "ritual humiliation"—a task or tasks that the adolescent will invariably fail or that will at least cause pain. This has a double purpose: first, to show the boy that he is not the center of the world; and second, to show him that failure and suffering are part of human life. Isn't that marvelous? As Rohr says, our culture has nothing like this. Our boys are programmed to believe that they must excel, be perfect, feel no pain, and never fail. No wonder we have so many teens suffering from depression and low self-esteem.

Rohr notes two other aspects of these male initiation rites. One is that they are always conducted by a group of mature men. At the end of the ritual, the men warmly and approvingly welcome the boy into "the company of men." Imagine what this does to confer a sense of masculinity on the young male. He is now "a man among men." He will be expected to work, to fight, to mate, to father and provide for children, and to contribute to the well-being of the community. He will sometimes fail, and he will have to suffer—but there is no shame in that. He is accepted, he belongs, he is fully *zakar*.

Another important purpose of the rite of passage is to put the boy in contact with the great myths, the sacred stories of his culture. Where did his people come from? What is their history? Who is their God (or gods)? What is their destiny as a people? In coming to understand these great truths, the young male gets a deep sense that he is indeed significant, but only as part of a larger world of purpose and meaning.

Contrast this rich experience with that of our own adolescents. Far from being welcomed into the company of adults, they are often disconnected from all but their own peer group. Instead of finding their place and their sense of worth in the sacred truths of the world's great religions, they look for it in the musical expressions and fashion statements of pop-culture figures. Rohr calls this "disaster"—from the Latin *astra* (stars) and the prefix "dis" (separated from)—"being disconnected from the stars," the heavens, the world of spiritual meaning. So all that's left is conformity to the codes of the peer group. The healing that comes from being welcomed into a caring community with a great story is missing.

When I shared some of these ideas at a recent retreat, the men did not totally agree that our culture has no rites of passage for adolescents. They noted, for example, certain key events in the life of teens: entrance into high school; getting the first regular job; obtaining a driver's license; being accepted into college or a desired job; turning eighteen. I had to agree with them, but I pointed out that none of these events is currently marked by any ritual, sacred or secular. I encouraged the retreatants to use their creativity in designing something.

One place to begin looking for ideas is Edward Hays's book *Prayers for the Domestic Church*.

The Need for Regulation

We have seen that *zakar* signifies the male's sexual endowment and sexual energy. It gives him a sense of gender identity as well as an awareness of a sacred connection with God. Unfortunately, many males in our society do not experience this healthy masculine energy and its sacred significance. This is partly because we have lost the connection between sexuality and spirituality, and partly because our society has no clear rituals to mark the stage of puberty.

But even if we can succeed in reclaiming the goodness and sacredness of phallic energy, that energy will always need to be disciplined and regulated. Otherwise, it can become a driving taskmaster. Human experience shows abundantly that, left to itself, sexuality can become demonic. Psychologist Rollo May has recalled for us the ancient Greek notion of the demonic, not in the sense of diabolical, but as "that which has the power to totally dominate our personality." In that sense, every addiction is demonic. And surely sex has that power to dominate us. As Hicks puts it:

> Without proper teaching on the phallus, men will carry around in their psyches a spiritual god-hunger so mysterious and powerful that when driven underground, it will seek spiritual fulfillment only in the secrecy of motel rooms, adult videos, and in the bragging and joking about sexual exploits in athletic locker rooms. For many men in our culture, the secrecy has driven them to gay bars, topless nightclubs, and endless secret affairs. This sexual energy, which is essentially spiritual, takes place under the cover of darkness, perhaps because the Church has not shed enough light on the spiritual nature of our sexuality. Therefore, our sexual compulsions, addictions, and aberrations have become our expressions of worship—worship of a false god

(Hicks 1993, 55).

Against a long-standing attitude of "anything goes" when it comes to sex, the Scriptures insist that sex needs to be regulated and channeled in accord with the plan of God for human fulfillment and happiness. In place of sex for recreation, the Bible holds up sex for relationship; that is, sexual activity needs an adequate *context* to give it meaning. Pleasure is certainly one of the purposes of sexual behavior, but without some meaning beyond pleasure, sex easily can be abused and dehumanized. The results include hurt feelings, broken marriages, neglected children, sexual abuse and violence, abortion, and AIDS.

While teaching an adult education class on Christian sexuality, I began by asking the participants (all laity) this question: "From a purely human standpoint, what values should be present in any sexual activity?" The answers they gave included "mutual respect," "love and care," "trust," "sensitivity to each other's needs," "commitment," and "children." I was thrilled. With those values firmly in mind, it is easy to see why the biblical and church teaching on sexuality makes sense. Once you remove sexual activity from its God-intended context—that is, committed, monogamous marriage—you jeopardize those deep human values that "good sex" should embody. I have since used this same approach with a group of college students as well as a high school confirmation class. Both groups came up with the same basic set of human values.

Let's examine this a little more closely. There is good reason to believe that the crisis of sexual morality today is not just a lack of clear norms. It goes much deeper than that. The real crisis is over the very meaning of human sexuality. And that is precisely why we must not dissociate sex from sin. To deprive sexual conduct of the possibility of sin is to render it trivial. Where no sin is possible, nothing is at stake. Put another way, as soon as values are at stake, sin becomes a possibility, because sin is the negation of a value, or at least a disordering of values. When we remove meaning, sex is bound to become empty and boring at best, or an instrument of exploitation at worst.

What Makes Sex Meaningful?

I recall a story I read in the paper about two female students at the Massachusetts Institute of Technology who published a "Consumer Guide to MIT Men." They rated the sexual performance of thirty-six male students, awarding each between zero and four stars. They rated the men by name and included descriptions of their technique, physical attributes, and personal hygiene. The women said they had based their ratings "on personal experience." Understandably, there was an uproar on campus. Students and faculty alike were outraged at the total insensitivity of the two female students. One of them tried to defend herself by saying that her intent was to show how women feel "when expected to perform for men."

While this rejoinder may not justify what the student did, it certainly hits home. Undoubtedly many men will recall their own experience of rating women. While it may not always go to the extreme described in this incident, it's a game we often play. What that incident brought home to me was how cruel sexual activity can become when it is divorced from a context of love and care. It is an extreme example, but it differs only in degree from the kinds of hurtful things that can happen when people engage in casual sex. Many are the ministers, therapists, and friends who have listened to stories of heartbreak from people who gave themselves sexually, only to find that the words of love spoken before and during the act were empty and manipulative.

What makes sex meaningful? I believe that the only adequate context for meaningful sex can be expressed in a few simple principles: sex needs love; sex needs commitment; sex is for new life.

Let's look at the first of these simple statements: "Sex needs love." As men, we recognize that it is very easy to separate our sex drive from our feelings. Our hormones drive us in this direction, and there is much in our culture that supports this. But if we look at ourselves not simply from the perspective of our biology, we recognize that we are more than our sex drive. As we reflect on our experience of sexual relationships we recognize that they involve powerful emotions as well, our own as well as those of others. Sexual involvement creates a great deal of vulnerability. Without love, the potential for hurt in a relationship is tremendous.

Love, of course, is more than mere words and deeper than feelings. Words and the feelings of love can pass. What happens when your partner no longer seems so appealing? What do you do when you find someone who can better fulfill your needs? Or what if you just plain get bored? How many people have been devastated by those chilling words, "I'm sorry, but I just don't love you any more"?

This leads us to our second simple statement about sex: "Sex needs commitment." It has often been noted that sex is a language. It gives bodily expression to some inner reality. When two people join their bodies in such profound intimacy, they are not only saying to each other, "I love you," but also, "I belong to you." And vice-versa, "you belong to me." This is not in the sense of ownership, but in the sense of partnership. But we are not truly partners, we do not truly belong to each other, unless there is a commitment between us: I promise to be true to you, to stay with you, to care about you—not just "as long as it feels right," but for as long as we live. Without that stability, that sense of permanence, sexual intercourse does not express the truth that love requires commitment.

While in prison, shortly before his execution by the Nazis, Lutheran pastor Dietrich Bonhoeffer wrote a wedding sermon for a young couple he knew. Stressing the positive connection between love and marriage, he said, "From now on, it is not your love which sustains the marriage, but the marriage that sustains your love." I like the point he made, but I would put it a little differently: "It is *both* your love that sustains your marriage and the marriage commitment that sustains your love."

Anyone who is married knows this. You need love and commitment to sustain a marriage. In times of illness or financial strain, when things aren't going right between a couple, or when there is a serious problem dividing them—in short—when the feeling of love is not present, it is the commitment that sustains the marriage. On the other hand, when a small gesture of thoughtfulness is offered, when forgiveness for a hurt is given without reservation, or when something happens to make one keenly aware of the love, then that feeling of love deepens and enriches the commitment.

It is in this context of the couple's whole life together, "in good times and in bad," that sexual love reaches the fullest expression of its meaning. Bishop John McGann of the Diocese of Rockville Centre in New York expresses the fact that sexual love is an integral part of marriage in his pastoral letter "Celebrate God's Gift of Sexuality":

> Many couples have told me that their sexual intimacy is a time of tenderness, of passion, of pleasure, and of celebration. Both husbands and wives have told me that, at times, making love to their spouse brings forgiveness, healing, and a profound sense of renewal to their relationship. This is what the church teaches about God's gift of sexuality, it is holy, powerful, life-giving, and demands our honest and faithful response (*Crux*, Jan. 22, 1996, 5).

When church teaching on sex is presented well and understood correctly, I think it makes a lot of sense. It is not negative about sex; it simply wants to uphold those deep human values that sexual activity ought to embody. The basic message is that sex works best when it takes place in the context of a loving, stable marriage. Outside of that context, it falls short of its God-intended purposes.

There is one more affirmation that needs to be made here, namely: "sex is for new life." Obviously I'm not saying that every married couple must produce a flock of children for their sexuality to be meaningful. Some form of birth control can be a truly moral option for couples. But sexual activity by its very nature includes a radical openness to the creation of new life. By "radical openness" I mean two things: 1) that the couple does not positively exclude children from their marriage; and 2) that they do not allow material values to so dominate their life that they crowd out all other values—including the desire to share their lives with children and give them the best of their care. It seems to me that if this attitude is absent in sexual expression, the couple can become more and more entrapped in mutual egoism. Sexuality finds its meaning in the fact that it is shared; and the ultimate in sharing is the procreation of new human life.

The life-giving dimension of sexual love involves not only the couple and their children, but the community and the society in which they live as well. The purpose of marriage is not only the good of the couple and their children, but for the sake of the whole community. The power and energy of sexual love within marriage can strengthen a man to be creative, compassionate, and generous to those in need. This too is new life.

I have tried to show that the biblical regulation of human sexuality can be summed up in three positive affirmations: "sex needs love"; "sex needs commitment"; "sex is for new life." I realize that this vision represents an ideal that is difficult to uphold in practice. Human beings will often fall short. Nowadays especially, when marriage has to be postponed for years until educations are completed and jobs are secured, and when so many cultural pressures are urging sexual expression, people will often find it very hard to postpone sex unless and until they can marry.

But what is the alternative? To abandon the ideal for one that is easier or more convenient? I don't think that's the answer. For one thing, it would not be faithful to the witness of both Scripture and Tradition. Moreover, any other approach to sexuality will generate even more problems than trying to uphold extramarital chastity. I think the church is very wise in continuing to uphold the traditional vision for human sexuality, to bless and affirm its goodness only within the bounds of committed marriage. In doing so we are fully aware that we will often fail to live up to the ideal. That is why we have the whole movement of repentance and forgiveness, the great journey of conversion that we are called to make over and over again.

The biblical *zakar* was often a man who failed to regulate his phallic energy according to the design of God. But he did not rationalize or justify his failure. He repented of it, and found the mercy of God waiting for him. Sexual sins are far from being the worst in the hierarchy of wrongdoing. Far worse, it seems to me, is to create one's own code of sexual ethics to suit one's convenience, or to accept the "anything goes" mentality of the surrounding culture.

Sex and the Single Male

Until now, my reflections on *zakar* have been focused largely within the context of marriage. I am aware, however, that some of my readers will be men who are currently single; not yet married, divorced, widowed, or gay men who are trying to live out the church's teaching regarding homosexual acts. What meaning does the biblical *zakar* have for them? How can they be whole persons without genital sexual expression?

I don't think there is an easy way to answer these questions, but let me make the best attempt I can. I think we need to begin with the assertion that sexual activity is not an absolute for human fulfillment. Years ago, the great humanistic psychologist Abraham Maslow did his famous study of "self-actualizing" people—those who embodied the best of human achievement and personal fulfillment. To his surprise, he found a few individuals in the sample who were living celibate lives. After studying these individuals more closely, Maslow came to the following conclusion:

It is now well known that there are many cases in which

celibacy has no psycho pathological effects. In many other cases, however, it has many bad effects. What factor determines which shall be the result? Clinical work with non-neurotic people gives a clear answer that sexual deprivation becomes pathogenic in a severe sense only when it is felt by the individual to represent rejection by the opposite sex, inferiority, lack of worth, isolation, or other thwarting of basic needs. Sexual deprivation can be borne with relative ease by individuals for whom it has no such implication (Quoted in Goble 1970, 78).

In other words, it is the *meaning* I attach to sexual abstinence that makes all the difference. If I freely choose to refrain from sex for reasons that are meaningful to me, my psycho/spiritual growth will not suffer. But if I avoid sex because of shame, fear of rejection, anger, or any other negative motivation, my sexual abstinence will become dysfunctional. It is not abstinence as such, but the meaning behind it, that is crucial.

Another way of saying it: it is love that matters, not sex. If I am able to find love in my life, I can find wholeness and fulfillment, whether or not I give it sexual expression. So I would like to say to all single males: nothing can stop you from loving. You can develop close, mutually enriching friendships with both sexes. With the power of prayer and the grace of God you can live a chaste lifestyle. Your life—every male's life—is bigger than the phallus. A true *zakar* is not one who is fixated on his sexual powers, but one who is able to channel his sexual energy into forms of love and creative endeavors. Many homosexuals and unmarried males are remarkably talented in the arts, in business, in social service occupations, in science and medicine. And they are striving to live a genuinely Christian spirituality. They are surely bearing the image of God in our world.

In summary, we can say that the *zakar* male is one who treasures his God-given phallic energy and strives to regulate it in accord with God's plan for sexuality. Typically awakened in adolescence, he finds loving and life-giving ways to express his sexual energy throughout the life-cycle. It thus becomes his good servant rather than his demanding master.

Four

WARRIOR MAN: CHOOSING YOUR BATTLES

We have seen that an important developmental stage in a man's life is learning to deal constructively with his sexual energy. We also said that there are too many men who fail to do this; instead, they become fixated on their phallus, forever trying to prove their virility by sexual exploits and conquests.

Healthy males, however, recognize that there is more to life than sex. There is work to be done and tasks to be achieved, knowledge to be gained, worlds to explore, obstacles to be overcome in the pursuit of worthwhile goals. For this men need another kind of energy, the kind denoted by the third Hebrew word for man, *gibbor*, usually translated "warrior."

Meaning of *Gibbor*

Robert Hicks suggests that the root idea present in *gibbor* is that of "power or strength with an emphasis on excellence and superiority." It connotes "gaining the upper hand," "to be prominent, important, distinguished." It is as if the sexual energy of the phallic male has been channeled into vocational pursuits: competing to be superior, using his energy to achieve and become prominent. In the Hebrew Scriptures, it commonly refers to military heroes or others who have shown great bravery. Joshua's and Saul's soldiers were all *gibbor* warriors. David was the ultimate *gibbor*; he slew the giant Goliath and rebuilt a ragtag militia into a large army, thereby bringing peace and security to the land. Later he formed a handpicked, elite squad of warriors to protect Jerusalem and the royal palace.

As time went on, however, *gibbor* also came to describe those who were spiritual warriors. "Better than *gibbor* strength is wisdom," we read in Ecclesiastes 9:16. And in Jeremiah:

> Thus says the Lord:
> "Let not . . . the strong man (*gibbor*) glory in his strength,
> But rather, let him who glories, glory in this,
> that in his prudence he knows me" (Jer 9:22-23).

Spiritual wisdom and knowledge of God and the ways of God were seen as more powerful in attaining true greatness than either physical strength or military genius.

The Warrior in Contemporary Society

It took me awhile to become comfortable with the warrior image. For one thing, it is too easily associated with war and violence, increasing concerns in our society. As early as 1963, Pope John XXIII declared that "war is no longer an appropriate means of repairing injustice." The Second Vatican Council unequivocally condemned the arms race. We recall the powerful words of Pope Paul VI in his address to the United Nations: "If you want to be brothers and sisters, let the weapons fall from your hands. You cannot love with weapons in your hands!" And thirty years later, in October 1995, Pope John Paul II made a similar plea on the fiftieth anniversary of the UN.

Why then am I willing to hold up the warrior as a positive image for contemporary males? Are not too many men too aggressive already? The daily papers are filled with accounts of shooting, fighting, sexual assault, and all manner of violence—most of it perpetrated by males. Hasn't competitiveness become an aggressive way of life for too many men—from the athletic field to the office, and even into domestic life? Sam Keen shows vividly how the language of the battlefield has been taken into the corporate world. He quotes the dust jacket of a book titled *Waging Business Warfare:*

> Believe it—if you're in business, you're at war. Your enemies—your competitors—intend to annihilate you. Just keeping your company alive on the battlefield is going to be a struggle. Winning may be impossible— unless you're a master of military strategy. . . . You can be—if you'll follow the examples of the great tacticians of history. Because the same techniques that made Genghis Khan, Hannibal, and Napoleon the incomparable conquerors they were are still working for. . . (the) super-strategists on today's corporate killing-fields. . . . Join them at the command post! Mastermind the battle! Clobber the enemy! Win the war! (Keen 1991, 59-60).

It is often said that language shapes behavior. When warlike language is used in the workplace (other examples include "corporate raiders," "hostile takeovers," "head-hunting," "making a killing"), it reinforces the tendency to see life as an unending battle wherein only the tough and aggressive will survive.

What does this kind of atmosphere do to a man's moral and spiritual sensitivity? Besides stress and burnout, he is likely to carry this attitude toward power, control, and competition into his marriage and the messages he gives, verbal and nonverbal, to his children. A few years ago Gary Abrams wrote an article in the *Los Angeles Times* entitled, "Did We Rear a Bunch of Moral Mutants?" His research found that 75 percent of high school students and 50 percent of college students admit to cheating in their school work. In business, 12 to 30 percent of job applications contain "deliberate inaccuracies." Abrams foresees "legions of young job applicants claiming degrees they don't have to get jobs they aren't qualified for . . . a tooth-and-nail scramble for economic survival, reward and prestige that will trample proper conduct, honesty and altruism." His conclusion: "This generation is the price we are paying for our own moral deterioration" (quoted in Cole 1992, 97-98).

A Positive Warrior Image

But granting all the negative possibilities and distortions inherent in the warrior image, is there any potential for healthy masculine energy here? I believe there is. We need to recall that *gibbor* was a very positive word for men in the Hebrew Scriptures. It was not used of the male who fought, plundered, and destroyed to show off his manliness or to enrich his own coffers. Rather, *gibbor* described the man who put his strength and courage at the service of God and the community. He felt called to protect his family and his nation from hostile invaders. He did not run away from obstacles or give up in the face of setbacks. He was willing to endure and struggle for a cause he believed in. He relied not on his own strength or cleverness, but on the power and guidance of the God he served.

There is something invigorating about this healthy warrior energy. Robert Bly fears that too many men today have lost this energy: "The warriors inside American men have become weak in recent years. . . . A grown man six feet tall will allow another person to cross his boundaries, enter his psychic house, verbally abuse him, carry away his treasures and slam the door behind; the invaded man will stand there with an ingratiating, confused smile on his face" (Bly 1990, 146). Psychologist Robert Moore says that behind every competent man is an active warrior who recognizes what is really important and doesn't get sidetracked by that which only glitters and distracts. In other words, he is focused on what matters. Jesuit Patrick Arnold, writes:

> The Warrior is one of the most important archetypes in masculine spirituality. . . . [W]arring is not only an occupation of great armies set off against one another across the trenches. It has become the masculine psychological paradigm for opposition to every evil: we battle disease, attack problems, combat drugs, struggle with ignorance, fight fires, and make war on poverty. Over the millennia, the Warrior has become in

the collective unconscious the archetype of resistance to evil in its myriad forms; lauded by poems, songs, and stories; celebrated and sanctified by rituals and blessed by the gods, the Warrior has come to epitomize the noblest qualities of masculinity: bravery, self-sacrifice, stamina, and heroic detachment (Arnold 1991, 101).

Let us look at our own experience. We can think of the good feeling we had as boys when we could "hold our own" in a dispute, could endure the fourteen-mile hike as Boy Scouts, or keep practicing diligently until we made the swim team. We recall how grateful we were when our dad, an older brother, or an uncle pushed and encouraged us to attempt some feat because they believed in us more than we did in ourselves.

Robert Hicks's father was general manager of Beech Aircraft Corporation and had a single-engine plane for his use. Hicks describes accompanying his dad on some of his flights. One day, when he was twelve years old, his dad taxied the plane to the runway, did all the pre-flight operations, and then said to Robert, "I think you're big enough to take this off." Hicks was thrilled. "Even though I was scared to death," he says, "the belief that my Dad trusted me with not only this airplane but also with his life gave me a surge of warrior courage. I reasoned: If my Dad thinks I am old enough, then I must be. I pulled back on the throttle, raced the plane down the runway, and pulled back on the stick. When we were airborne, I felt like I had had my *bar mitzvah*. That's the day my Dad looked upon me as a man" (Hicks 1993, 93).

Hicks believes that developing a sense of the warrior is a necessary step in the male journey. The normal timeframe stretches between adolescence and thirty-something. This is when most young men are acquiring their education and striving to establish themselves. It requires a great deal of energy and stamina to work for good grades in school, fill out job applications and hold interviews, perform well on the job, know when to take risks and when to hold steady, and stand up for one's rights when they are at stake.

On the other hand, if we repress the warrior, we are in danger of taking on the role of victim—whining about how bad off we are, how everyone dumps on us, how life is unfair—consuming ourselves with self-pity but taking no constructive action to change anything. Such men are pitiful indeed. In their passivity they appear to be beaten down by life. They are depressed and full of resentments. We wish they would "stand up and fight like a man" for what is rightfully theirs. Instead, they have settled for life in a rut, fearful of making waves. I once heard a quote from Garrison Keillor: "You taught me to be nice; and now I'm so nice that I have no outrage, no passion." How sad. Healthy warrior energy is a way to become an agent rather than a victim in the drama of life.

Forms of Warrior Energy

If we are in touch with the healthy *gibbor* within us, how do we act? For one thing, we are assertive when the situation calls for it. We move out of a passive, defensive stance and are willing to confront the challenges and problems that life presents. In the choice between fight or flight, we decide to stand our ground, to speak up for what we believe is right. We are willing to accept the consequences. "The fight matures," Hicks says, "and the drawing of psychic blood develops the young phallic male into a *gibbor*."

We have all had experiences like this—times when we stood up to parents, held firm when pressured to give in to children's demands, refused to keep covering up for our boss or for some irresponsible coworker. I once heard Richard Rohr talk about "the Sacred *no*"—whereby we set boundaries and limits on people or policies that make unreasonable demands on us. Without the sacred *no*, he says, nothing is forbidden; and therefore nothing is required. There is no clear sense of right and wrong. If I am unable to say no to anything, my yes is merely mechanical and compulsive. It will be neither wholehearted nor joyous. I will do the task, but it will be with resentment and/or self-pity—the breeding grounds of depression.

The truth is, we often have to defend our psychic space against people butting into our lives, putting us down, making offensive remarks, trying to push us around. "Hardly a day goes by," Patrick Arnold says, "that we don't need to draw the Warrior's sword and flash it in the face of this busybody or that boor, this rude waiter or that prying relative" (Arnold 1991, 103). We don't need to *use* the sword, Arnold adds; it is sufficient just to show it in order to indicate where the boundaries are.

Another manifestation of *gibbor* strength is self-discipline. The messages of contemporary culture pull us in the opposite direction toward softness, ease, and self-indulgence, but the warrior in us knows better. He understands that discipline of mind and body are absolutely required for spiritual growth.

> Whether you're literally a hunter, crouched for hours in the chill early morning waiting for your prey to come within range, or a triathlon trainee, a medical school student, an executive enduring the misguided attacks of your board members, or a husband trying to work out difficulties with your wife—you *know* that discipline of your mind and body are essential" (Moore 1990, 75).

Moore reminds us that we all have competing claims on our time and energy. So the warrior in us helps us to set priorities and stick with tasks despite their distastefulness and our own weariness.

The Importance of Values

Granted that our inner warrior can provide us with the energy to be assertive and self-disciplined in the pursuit of our goals, a key question still remains: what is worth fighting for? On what basis do we decide which competing claims on our time and energy will merit our attention and investment? It is tragic to see men who appear to fight for the sake of fighting. As Hicks says,

> The challenge of being a warrior is twofold: knowing what to fight for, and knowing when to quit. . . . We certainly need warriors for the truth, to fight for the spiritual values in our society before they become extinct. But we also see many who war needlessly, or war for causes that are far removed from the category of "worth dying for" (Hicks 1993, 95).

This raises the question of values and priorities. Many contemporary social philosophers have noted that we live in a culture that values individualism. The one value that seems to underlie all choices is individual freedom. We believe that everyone ought to enjoy the freedom to choose whatever is personally satisfying. But often little or no thought is given to what might be good or better for someone else or for the wider community. Here is where we see the shadow side of the warrior: the man who aggressively pursues his own self-interest without regard for the rights or feelings of other people; the compulsive workaholic who can't relax or play or take time for intimate relationships with family and friends; or the burned-out crusader who doesn't know how to choose his battles.

Christians have always claimed that personal gain and personal satisfaction are legitimate pursuits, but are not of themselves adequate guides for making choices. There are values that transcend individual self-interest. Both Hebrew and Christian Scriptures reveal a value structure that points us beyond ourselves. They make it clear that some values are more worthy of our loyalty than others:

- ◆ Speaking the truth is better than deception.

- ◆ Treating people with kindness is better than cruelty.

- ◆ Fulfilling responsibilities is better than reneging on them.

◆ Affirming people is better than ridiculing them.

◆ Respecting people's property is better than stealing.

◆ Using time and talents productively is better than wasting them.

◆ Taking proper care of our health is better than neglecting it.

◆ Respecting the freedom of others is better than controlling them for our own advantage.

◆ Sex with love and commitment is better than casual sex.

A truly spiritual *gibbor* exercises discipline, not for its own sake, but for the sake of actualizing goals and values that he has personally assimilated. These values give direction to his life and empower him to make decisions even in the face of competing pressures.

The Virtue of Courage

A final quality of the warrior is that he is developing the virtue of courage, or what the Bible and Christian tradition have often called "fortitude." I find it fascinating to read the gospels and see how Jesus often draws upon his warrior energy. The most obvious example is the scene where he drives the money-changers out of the Temple:

> He found in the temple area those who sold oxen, sheep, and doves, as well as the money-changers seated there. He made a whip out of cords and drove them all out of the temple area, with the sheep and the oxen, and spilled the coins of the money-changers and overturned their tables, and to those who sold doves he said, "Take these out of here, and stop making my Father's house a marketplace" (Jn 2:14-16).

This is not the soft and gentle Jesus we often hold in our imaginations. This is the *gibbor* Jesus, fighting for the rights of the poor pilgrims and for the dignity of God's house of prayer. And when challenged by the religious authorities for his behavior, he refused to back down or apologize.

Nor is this the only example of warrior courage in the gospels. Very early in Mark's account we see Jesus acting with remarkable assertiveness. Shortly after he called Levi (Matthew) to be a disciple, Levi held a banquet at his house for his friends: tax collectors and those known as sinners. The Pharisees complained to the disciples (note how they don't speak directly to Jesus), "Why does he eat with tax collectors and sinners?" Jesus overheard the sneering remark and didn't let it pass: "Those who are well do not need a physician, but the sick do. I did not come to call the righteous but sinners" (Mk 2:15-17). That takes courage.

The next chapter begins with another story that contrasts the passive-aggressive attitude of the Pharisees with the healthy assertiveness of Jesus. He was teaching in the synagogue, and a man with a withered hand was there in the audience. Jesus' opponents were watching him closely, "so that they might accuse him." Jesus asked the man to come forward. Then he spoke directly to his opponents, "Is it lawful to do good on the sabbath rather than to do evil, to save one life rather than to destroy it?" What a disarmingly simple question. Anyone with an open mind and common sense should have been able to answer it. But "they remained silent." Another passive-aggressive gesture, which stirred up Jesus' *gibbor* energy: "he was looking around at them with anger and grieved at their hardness of heart." Note the strong language: "anger," "grieved." Jesus did not stifle his emotions. Rather, he allowed them to surface and directed them to the service of his values. After this silent but unmistakable rebuke to his adversaries, he directed his attention back to the suffering man and asked him simply to stretch out his withered hand. "He stretched it out and his hand was restored." Jesus did not allow the narrowness and hostility of men jealous of their position to thwart his own compassion and healing power (Mk 3:1-5).

A couple of scenes later, Jesus expelled a demon from a man who was mute. Instead of glorifying God for this wondrous event, his opponents again began picking at him. This time they accused him of being in league with Satan, of receiving the power to cast out demons from him. Jesus immediately confronted them, pointing out how ridiculous such an accusation was: why would one devil try to cast out another devil? "And if Satan is divided against himself, how will his kingdom stand?" (Lk 11:14-18; cf. Mk 3:22-24). I find it highly instructive to reflect on passages like these, because they show how one can be assertive without resorting to violence, whether physical or verbal.

Another lesson we learn from reading the Christian Scriptures is that Jesus wanted to imbue his followers with this kind of warrior courage. It is not the fruit of their own efforts or training, however, but a gift of the Holy Spirit. In the gospels the disciples often displayed a lot of good will, but their natural cowardice and lack of self-confidence always tripped them up. Only after the outpouring of the Holy Spirit at Pentecost, did they begin to act as spiritual warriors. When Peter and John were arrested for healing a crippled man, the authorities didn't know what to do with them; the ordinary people were ready to listen to the apostles' teaching about the crucified and risen Christ. "So they called them [the apostles] back and ordered them not to speak or teach at all in the name of Jesus." But Peter and John stood firm. "It is impossible for us not to speak about what we have seen and heard" (Acts 4:13-20). This is the kind of courage and fortitude that make us willing to suffer for a cause we believe in.

In the lives of most men there will probably be few if any occasions that call for heroic courage. But it seems to me that life is filled with situations that require us to draw upon this kind of *gibbor* strength. We need, for example, the courage to face and deal with problems. Too many men spend their energy trying to deny or avoid problems rather than solving them. Scott Peck reminded us that "life is a series of problems. Do we want to moan about them or solve them? Do we want to teach our children to solve them?" He went on to say: "Problems call forth our courage and our wisdom; indeed, they create our courage and our wisdom. It is only because of problems that we grow mentally and spiritually" (Peck 1978, 15-16).

Society reinforces our natural tendency to deny or avoid problems. For example, why do men as a group have more health problems and die at an earlier age than women? Part of the reason, I'm sure, is stress. But another reason is that men tend to deny their symptoms. For one thing, it's not macho to be sick. Besides, it's scary to think about what the doctors might find. So we slip into denial.

Denial and avoidance are often operative in other areas of life. A man may be miserable on the job. He will complain to his wife and to anyone else who will listen, but he will not talk to his supervisor or anyone else who could actually do something about it. Why? Because he's afraid he will lose face, or he will be looked upon as a troublemaker. Fear is the real enemy. Or a marriage may show clear signs of deteriorating, yet neither spouse will talk about it because it might be too painful. Perhaps the wife suggests going for counseling, but the husband insists that "we don't have any problems we can't solve ourselves." Here, denial is feeding on the macho image. Or when a child shows behavior problems, the father may tend to ignore them or dismiss them as nothing more than "growing pains."

Here is where we need to cultivate the inner warrior. The truth is that taking responsibility for solving our problems is the surest way to strengthen our self-esteem and to overcome our sense of powerlessness. As adults we tend to measure our worth by the symbols of success—money, possessions, occupational status. There is nothing intrinsically wrong with that. But it will not be enough unless we also have the satisfaction of knowing that we have tried our best to solve the problems that life has thrust upon us.

Finally, I want to return once more to the life of Jesus. We saw before how he drew upon *gibbor* energy to deal with those who kept opposing his ministry. But these skirmishes were only preparation for the finale: he would have to face rejection and the cross. Luke sets us up for the turning point when he writes: "When the days for his being taken up were fulfilled, he resolutely determined to journey to Jerusalem" (Lk 9:51). What a strong image of courage, of facing life's problems rather than running away from them. Three times Jesus tried to tell the disciples that they had to be ready for trouble, that he himself would have to undergo suffering and death. But each time the disciples went into denial (Mk 8:31-33; 9:30-32; 10:32-45). Jesus would not back down. In fact, he let the disciples know that they could not be his followers unless they were willing to take up their cross each day—that is, to face and deal with the conflicts, challenges, and problems of their lives as Christians.

Jesus knew that this would be hard so he assured his disciples that he would not leave them to struggle alone. At the Last Supper he told them: "In the world you will have trouble, but take courage, I have conquered the world" (Jn 16:33). He promised to send them the Holy Spirit, who would give them the power and the wisdom to overcome the problems they would have to face.

Christ made the same commitment to us. We are his disciples today, and we have received the Holy Spirit in our baptism and confirmation. We can count on the Spirit to help us in our efforts to act lovingly and courageously as we uphold the values we believe in and the people we care about. Being a good warrior does not mean being pushy, obnoxious, or aggressive. It does mean accepting our responsibility to make things happen. The Christian life is never an easy escape into pious longing for the next life; rather, it is a courageous taking of responsibility for the betterment of ourselves, our loved ones, and our world.

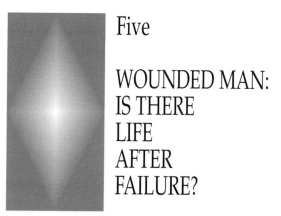

Five

WOUNDED MAN: IS THERE LIFE AFTER FAILURE?

When John F. Kennedy was shot, TV newsmen were everywhere, interviewing people about their reactions to the terrible event. One person interviewed was Daniel Moynihan, then a young member of the House of Representatives: "Congressman, how do you feel about this?" The big Irishman had tears in his eyes as he replied, "When you're Irish, one of the first things you learn is: sooner or later life will break your heart." I remember thinking that you don't have to be Irish to know that. It's the bare truth; life has a thousand ways of hurting us.

So it is with the *gibbor* male. Working hard to achieve his goals and dreams, find success, distinguish himself, win the esteem and recognition of others—eventually he stumbles and falls. The warrior takes a hit. And so we come to the fourth Hebrew word for man: *enosh* ("wounded").

Robert Hicks quotes several men describing their wounding experiences:

- ♦ "The day I killed my first Iraqi, something died within me." A paratrooper in the Persian Gulf War.

63

- ◆ "If I had known life was going to be so tough, I don't think I would have signed up for it." A fairly successful executive.

- ◆ "I'm finally realizing what lack of a father has really done to me." Another man.

Each of us can generate our own list of such experiences. During my very first year in the priesthood, the first two converts I instructed ended up marrying outside of the church, and the first couple I married both ended up in prison. Not a great start. One of my friends, in an effort at encouragement, sent me a small plaque for my desk that read: "If at first you don't succeed—you're about average!"

I think the reason poet Robert Bly has attracted so many different types of men to his retreats is that he so clearly names the pain that men are feeling but are not able to talk about. In the act of sharing his own woundedness (growing up with an alcoholic father), Bly gives men permission, so to speak, to feel their own pain. He calls it grief, and it stems from the losses that men experience along life's journey: loss of health, job losses, the breakup of a marriage, loss of status, loss of self-esteem because of mistakes and failures, death of loved ones. In order for men to discover what manhood is all about, they must descend into the deep places of their own souls and find their accumulated grief (Bly 1990, 27).

Meaning of *Enosh*

The Hebrew word *enosh* literally means "being weak, fragile." It connotes a human characteristic that we males don't easily accept: our vulnerability. We gladly celebrate our phallic energy and our warrior strength, but we don't like to think in terms of loss, limits, failure, and wounding. Yet the Bible will not allow us to live on illusion. The psalms, for example, abound in references to the rigorous truth of human fragility:

"Man's (*enosh*) days are like those of grass" (Ps 103:15).

"What is man (*enosh*), that you should be mindful of
    him?" (Ps 8:4).

"You turn man (*enosh*) back to dust" (Ps 90:3).

Still, the Bible does not view our vulnerability as a negative. Rather, awareness of our wounded condition is the surest
way to keep us grounded in reality. Contrary to the adolescent
fantasy, we are not invincible, not omnipotent. And contrary
to the cultural myth about maleness, we are not self-sufficient
either. We are going to get wounded by life, and we will need
others for our healing.

Sources of Wounding

I have already noted above one of the major sources of
wounding: our experiences of loss. Now I want to describe
what many in the men's movement today are calling "the
father wound." Richard Rohr has done a good deal of work
with this concept in his retreats. He notes that each of us comes
into this world biologically bonded to our mother. Her love
and presence are givens. But our father first enters our world
as a stranger. His acceptance or rejection of us is our first clue
as to whether the outer world can be trusted. For some
unknown reason, a smile or hug from the father is more affirming and energizing than the mother's constant love. Perhaps
this is because it is our first experience of election, of being
freely chosen. It is no accident, Rohr says, that Jesus called God
"Father." He knew it would be harder for us to believe in
father-love than in mother-love.

Before the Industrial Revolution, Robert Bly says, boys
received a sense of masculine identity just by standing next to
their fathers, working on the farm or in the family trade. It
was almost like a transfer of male energy from father to son.
But since the Industrial Revolution most fathers have had to
work away from home, and growing boys are deprived of that
natural father-bonding. Fortunately, many fathers are able to
find other ways to bond with their sons, such as playing

sports, working together around the house, taking walks in the woods, visiting to parks and zoos, reading together, and telling stories.

But what if the father is absent—either physically or emotionally? What if divorce, abandonment, or imprisonment has taken him out of the home? Or, if he is there, what if he is in the grip of alcohol or other addiction? Or so preoccupied with work that he has no time or energy for his children? Or is so critical of them that they can never win his approval? In such situations, Rohr speculates, the boy grows up with "a hole in the soul" through which demons can enter—the demons of anger, of mistrust of males, of wounded self-esteem.

My friend Lou Lussier speaks about what he calls "the silence of the father." That is, the father may be present in the home, not be critical or abusive, but is simply silent. He does not or cannot share his inner thoughts and feelings. He may be a good provider, but he gives little or nothing of who he is. The child experiences this as rejection: "I am not good enough to receive that part of my father." So the boy grows up not quite knowing what it means to be a male; he may latch onto any stereotype that happens to be around. Moreover, he is likely to continue the pattern when he becomes a father himself, because he has little healthy male energy to pass on to his own children.

Another source of male wounding is what Clayton Barbeau has called "the failure of success." He described an interesting case study. A twenty-three-year-old man (a typical young warrior) had resolved that by age forty-five he would have a wife and several children, two cars, a luxury home, and an income of at least $50,000 a year. The psychiatrist presenting the case said that the man succeeded in achieving all these goals, and even surpassing the financial one, by age forty-three. But at that point he began to drink excessively, indulge in reckless gambling, chase around with young women, and show other signs of personality disorder. Within two years his wife divorced him, and he was bankrupt. He entered the hospital with a diagnosis of major depression. The psychiatrist concluded his presentation by saying, "Now that's what I call the will to fail."

But Clayton Barbeau disagreed. He pointed out that not only had the man not failed to achieve his goals, but he had succeeded admirably, beating his own timetable by two years. What this case demonstrated, Barbeau said, was "the failure of success." Having fulfilled his dream, his very success failed him. It did not bring him the deep-down satisfaction he had been shaped to expect. He was disillusioned with the great American dream (Barbeau 1982, 75-76).

Stephen Covey makes the same point in *Seven Habits of Highly Effective People*. It's incredibly easy, he says, "to work harder and harder at climbing the ladder of success only to discover it's leaning against the wrong wall." Once you get to the top, you find there's nothing on the other side. "People often find themselves achieving victories that are empty, successes that have come at the expense of things they suddenly realize were far more valuable to them . . . that their drive to achieve their goal blinded them to the things that really mattered most and are now gone" (Covey 1990, 98). This is indeed a great wounding. Often it manifests itself as a deep loneliness. Having been overinvested in activity and accomplishment, the man has not taken time to nurture mutually enriching relationships with people.

Typical Responses to Wounding

One of the ways to deal with the wounds inflicted by life is to deny the pain. This is particularly typical of younger males. They are too busy running in the fast track and having fun to notice that they are bleeding emotionally. As Hicks says, "They bury their wounds and bandage their bruises with put-on smiles, but wrestle with gaping holes in their souls." Or, perhaps many younger men simply don't experience wounding. I just finished giving a men's retreat at which there were a few men in their twenties. After my presentation on *enosh*, I invited the men to share in small groups their experiences of wounding. Interestingly, the younger men said they could not recall any. But they appreciated hearing the other men's stories and the lessons they had acquired in the process of becoming *enosh* males.

When wounding cannot be denied, one common response is anger. "Life is unfair," the man laments. "It's not supposed to be this way." "Life is a bitch." "What's the use of knocking yourself out, if this is all you get for it." Like wounded animals, we withdraw into self-pity or quiet rage. Or we snarl against society, women, our bosses, or God. Such feelings are neither sinful nor unhealthy. If we pray the psalms or read the great stories of the Bible, we find that the friends of God often felt they were being cheated by life and had no hesitation about telling God just what they thought: "Why do you treat your servant so badly?" Moses cried out to the Lord (Nm 11:11). "Why, O God, have you cast us off forever?" says the troubled psalmist (Ps 74:1). Another psalm is a cry of doubt from one who wonders why the wicked prosper while he gets beaten down for trying to be good: "Is it but in vain I have kept my heart clean and washed my hands as an innocent man? For I suffer affliction day after day and chastisement with each new dawn" (Ps 73:13-14).

These are natural and normal reactions to the pain of wounding. What is important is what happens next. Do we stay stuck in anger and self-pity, or do we move—toward acceptance, toward growth in maturity and deeper spirituality, toward compassion for others who are wounded?

Another common response is to turn our anger in upon ourselves, blaming ourselves for the wound: "Why was I so stupid?" "Why wasn't I more careful?" "How could I have been so blind?" Again, this spontaneous reaction to our wounding need not be disastrous. But it does signal a need to move through shame and self-blame to self-forgiveness and healing. As Hicks puts it, we should begin to say to ourselves and to our wounded brothers: "Your wound is honorable. Your wound is a normal part of male development. Life is not over. This wound may be the entry point for new wisdom and power; it may be the voice of God. Now we need to figure out what it means and how to move toward healing in order to keep you on the masculine journey" (Hicks 1993, 108).

Positive Possibilities from Wounding

Can wounding be good for the soul? It was Robert Bly who made me aware that the theme of wounding as necessary for the spiritual journey is prominent in the great myths and fairy tales of world literature. He uses the image of descent. In contrast to the dominant myth of American society (upward mobility), folk literature makes it clear that the mythic hero always has to make a journey downward. He has to struggle against great odds, like the biblical *gibbor*, and he always gets scarred and wounded like *enosh*.

In the Iron John story, for instance, the young prince accompanies the wild man, Iron John, into the forest, where he learns all sorts of important lessons about physical endurance, the mysteries of nature, and human behavior. But at one point Iron John abandons him, telling him he must now make his own way in the world. So the boy has to get a job working in the kitchen of another castle—he makes his descent and receives his wound of humiliation (he is, after all, a prince). Yet in that lowly kitchen the young prince learns much about the ways of thinking, feeling, and suffering of ordinary peasants, knowledge which eventually enables him to be a wise and kindly king.

So, too, in the story of The Three Brothers and the Dwarfs, the youngest brother is the only one who is willing to make the dangerous descent into the bowels of the earth in order to rescue the lost princess. But then, in a selfish and treacherous act, the two older brothers refuse to fetch him back from the underworld and try to convince the king that *they* deserve the reward for rescuing the princess. Meanwhile, the youngest brother is left to spend eighteen months in the underworld. But there the dwarfs teach him all kinds of wisdom and practical skills, so that he can eventually return to the earth, make the truth known to all the realm, and marry the beautiful princess. Bly suggests that these stories reveal something deep in the human psyche that recognizes the necessity for wounding and descent for any kind of spiritual maturity.

I find it fascinating now to read the Scriptures through these lenses. I find so many biblical figures who have suffered wounding and grown through it. Moses grew up in softness and luxury in the palace of Egypt's pharaoh. When he finally ventured outside the royal palace, he was shocked to see how his own Hebrew people were being treated. He "woke up" to injustice, and with typical *gibbor* energy he killed the Egyptian who was beating a Hebrew slave. But when the incident became public, Moses had to flee to the barren land of Midian, where he got a job tending sheep. Note the descent. There he lived for a long period of time, "a stranger in a foreign land," forgotten and cut off from his people. But it was there, in that forsaken wilderness, that he received the revelation of God in the burning bush: "Come, now! I will send you to Pharaoh to lead my people, the Israelites, out of Egypt. . . I will be with you" (Ex 3:10-12).

Another biblical figure who was brought to greater spiritual maturity through wounding was Elijah. God gave Elijah the task of calling the people of Israel and their leaders out of their idolatry and immorality and back to their covenant relationship with God. At first Elijah had great success: his preaching and his miracles woke the people up and brought them to spiritual conversion. Eventually, however, he provoked the wrath of the civil and religious leaders, and they put out a contract to have him killed. Elijah had to flee for his life. He went to the desert (place of descent), threw himself down on the ground, and prayed to Yahweh for death: "This is enough, O Lord! Take my life, for I am no better than my fathers" (1 Kgs 19:4). Today we would say, "I've had it. I can't take any more!"

But in that very moment of darkness and apparent failure,

God spoke to Elijah in the depths of his heart. First, God refreshed him with food and drink. Then God directed him to go even further into the desert—to Mount Sinai, where it all began, where God first called the Hebrew people together and promised always to be their God, never to forsake them. And there God reassured Elijah that he had not really failed, that there were at least seven thousand people in the land of Israel who were still holding to their faith in God. So Elijah went back. He found a spiritual young man (Elisha) and taught him so he could continue the work after Elijah was taken up to heaven (cf. 1 Kgs 19:5-18). Elijah could have wallowed in his depression and self-pity. Instead, he accepted the wounding of the *enosh* male and emerged more of a spiritual *gibbor* than ever.

In fact, if we study the Scriptures more closely, we find that *all* the great warriors had to go through times of wounding. Jeremiah, for example, was a thorn in the side of his contemporaries because he kept challenging them on their unwillingness to face the moral and spiritual decay that was setting them up for material disaster. At one point he begged God to explain why he was being treated so badly: "Tell me, Lord, have I not served you for their good? Have I not interceded with you in the time of misfortune and anguish . . . ? Why is my pain continuous, my wound incurable, refusing to be healed?" God did not really explain—he seldom does. But the wounded warrior received this reassurance: "Though they fight against you, they shall not prevail; for I am with you" (Jer 15:10-20). "I am with you"—that is the constant word of assurance and encouragement from God to *enosh.*

The book of Job is the classic story of the good man who seemed to have everything going for him, including the blessing and favor of God. But then it all began to unravel. Loss after loss came upon Job—flocks and herds, sons and daughters, the love and respect of his wife, his own health. At first he tried to be brave, but finally he could hold in his grief no longer: "[S]ighing comes more readily to me than food, and my groans well forth like water. For what I fear overtakes me, and what I shrink from comes upon me. I have no peace nor ease; I have no rest, for trouble comes!" (Job 3:24-26).

Soon Job's well-intentioned but insensitive friends come to comfort him. But instead of encouragement, they try to convince him that his sufferings are God's punishment for his sins: they tell him to examine his conscience and "come clean." But Job continues to maintain his innocence and his dignity. In fact, his woundedness draws him into an even deeper confidence and trust in God. At one point he says to his friends, with strong conviction: "I know that my Vindicator lives, and that he will at last stand forth upon the dust; whom I myself shall see: my own eyes . . . shall behold him, and from my flesh I shall see God" (Job 19:25-27).

The Christian scriptures portray Jesus as entering most profoundly into the descent of *enosh*, a wounding that brought healing to all of us: "By his wounds you have been healed," St. Peter says (1 Pt 2:24). And St. Paul quotes an ancient Christian hymn proclaiming that Christ's descent into suffering and death was the very means whereby he was exalted in glory and became our Savior: "Though he was in the form of God, [he] did not regard equality with God something to be grasped. Rather, he emptied himself, taking the form of a slave . . . he humbled himself, becoming obedient to death, even death on a cross. Because of this, God greatly exalted him and bestowed on him the name that is above every name. . ." (Phil 2:6-9). According to Scripture, there was some kind of divine necessity about Jesus' suffering and death (see Lk 24:26), not in the sense that his suffering somehow placated an angry God, but in the sense that it revealed the full extent of God's compassionate love for us and showed us that our own wounding is a necessary passage on the spiritual journey.

Learn to Value the Things That Really Matter

If defeat, failure, and woundedness are inevitable parts of the human condition, what is their positive value? How can they benefit us spiritually? I believe there are several ways. For one thing, they can teach us detachment from that which is only transitory and relative. So much of our life can be consumed with things and experiences that our culture tells us are crucial for our happiness. Sometimes it is only through loss that we come to realize we have been deceived about what is truly important.

Here is a small example. Some years ago, when I was doing a lot of driving, my car had only an AM radio. So the only music I could get was pop, rock, and country, none of which had much appeal for me. I guess I must have complained frequently about this, because one day some friends bought me an FM tuner. Ah—for about a week I enjoyed the sounds of beautiful classical music. But then some hoodlums broke into my car and stole the radio. I was a basket case. I whined and ranted. I called down anathemas and ex-communications on these evil people. Finally I calmed down. "What's the matter with you?" I said. "Your possessions are starting to possess you. Is that what you want?" No—it wasn't. It was about that time, I think, that I began to realize that *very few things really matter.* I need to keep focused on those, and let go—mentally and emotionally—of those that do not.

I have met many people who have shared with me some of their deepest losses and woundings. Often, as they struggle and grieve over what has happened, they come to that place in their soul where they discover the lesson they are supposed to learn. What, after all, is really important? Very often, in the loss of job or material things, people end up saying, "But I still have my family and my friends." "We still have each other." I heard such statements over and over again from the people whose homes or cars were damaged in the terrible flood of 1986 in Saginaw, Michigan. They came to realize the profound truth that relationships, love, interpersonal bonds are far more precious than anything material.

Recently I saw the movie *A Walk in the Clouds*. At the end of the film a raging fire destroys all the grapevines the Mexican-American family has worked so hard to cultivate. As they give vent to their grief, they come to realize that all of them are still alive, that no one is hurt. Not only that, but the pride and arrogance of the father are burned away as he recognizes how much he loves his wife and children and even the new son-in-law he had detested out of sheer prejudice. Finally, as they walk through the ruins, they spot one fresh sprig of a vine growing at the graveside of the grandfather— a symbol of new hope. They will begin again.

Sometimes when loss or wounding occur, people will say, "We still have our health." But what if the loss is precisely that—loss of health? That is a hard wound to bear. I remember the grief of my family when Dad was diagnosed with a terminal illness. For the next four years our mother took care of him at home, with the help of the other family members. It was a time of deep descent for all of us, especially as Dad's mind and speech began to fail. But out of that experience grew a strong bond of love and care among all of us, a deeper appreciation of the simple joys of being together as a family, bonded together by our common pain. Later, when Mom's health failed, we walked that path once again, with the same spirit of love and care for her and growing closeness with one another.

There is a line in one of St. Paul's letters that I have come to treasure: "This is my prayer: that . . . [you may] discern what is of value" (Phil 1:9-10). What a fine prayer. I try to make it my own, especially when I suffer loss or wounding. What, after all, really matters? To know, love, and serve God. To love and care for other people. To be true to my word, faithful to my commitments. To use my gifts and talents to bring something of God's love and healing into the lives of hurting people. To leave this world a little better place because I was part of it. Nothing and nobody can take any of that away from me.

So, it is often through loss and failure that a man becomes an *enosh* male. I have always admired St. Thomas More in this regard. More was a man who "had it all": personal friendship with the king of England, high government position, devoted wife and children, comfortable lifestyle. But he lost it all when he refused to take the oath of loyalty acknowledging the king as supreme head of the church. For that he was imprisoned and eventually beheaded. In the darkness of that great descent, he spoke a prayer of profound gratitude and detachment: "O Lord, I thank you for all you have given me. I thank you for all you have taken away. And I thank you for all I still have left." Here was a man who lost every worldly good, but he had learned to value the things that really matter. He still had his integrity. He had the peace of a clear conscience. And he had the firm hope of eternal life.

Open to God's Healing

Another value of the wounding experience is that it can open us up to the healing power of God. The original sin of *'adam* was the arrogant desire to become the equal of God, to have total control over life and destiny, to be accountable to no one. One of the insights of Alcoholics Anonymous is that this is one of the well-springs of addiction: the drug makes users feel powerful, in control, superhuman. "Before all else," they say, "we have to stop playing God." When their descent into the hell of addiction becomes painful enough, alcoholics finally cry out for help. AA teaches them to trust not in themselves, but in their Higher Power; to surrender their lives to the care of God; to stop trying to be perfect and allow God's grace to heal them.

It is the same with each of us in the *enosh* stage of our journey. Our experience of failure and wounding unmasks our pretenses of power, unlimited potential, and invulnerability. It is often a major conversion moment. We make a turn toward God, and we find that God is there waiting for us with unconditional love. As Abraham Lincoln once said, "I have been driven many times to my knees by the overwhelming conviction that I had nowhere else to go." Kurtz and Ketcham put it this way: "Our imperfection is the crack that lets God in . . . God comes in through our wound" (Kurtz and Ketcham 1992, 28). Even our sins and wrong choices, paradoxically, can bring us closer to God. The authors go on to share a beautiful image from the fifteenth-century mystic Meister Eckhart. He says that God has each of us on a string. When we sin, we cut the string. But when we repent, God knots the string. Then we sin again, repent, and once again God ties a knot in the string. But what's happening? Each time the string gets shorter, and we grow closer to God.

That very message Jesus tried to give us in so many ways:

> "Those who are healthy do not need a physician, but the sick do" (Lk 5:31).

> "The Son of Man has come to seek and to save what was lost" (Lk 19:10).

> "I did not come to call the righteous but sinners" (Mt 9:13).

And he told the story of the prodigal son. It was only after the young man "bottomed out" that he came to his senses and returned home—to find his father waiting for him with forgiveness and a chance to begin again.

Move Toward Solidarity

Finally, it is often through our experience of wounding that we begin to let go of our competitiveness. We start to recognize that there is a vast difference between striving for excellence and feeling compelled to beat everyone else in the endeavor of the moment. We come to acknowledge the high price we are paying for acquiring the competitive edge: stress-related illnesses, strained marriages, emotional distance from children and friends, lack of time and energy for nourishing our souls.

So the *enosh* male makes a move toward solidarity rather than competition. He sees that it is less important to be "one up" than "side by side." After all, the ancient Christian belief is that we belong to a communion of saints as well as to the fellowship of sinners. Americans cling tenaciously to the values of privacy, independence, and individualism, but at the same time they feel a deep loneliness and a hunger for community, for connectedness. This need or feeling, however, is often repressed during the years of warrior striving and achievement. It is only when the *gibbor* male "takes the hit" or "has the fall" that he feels in his gut the pain of being isolated and out of community.

So where does he turn for solidarity? Sometimes to his wife or girlfriend. Sometimes to a male friend. Sometimes to a psychotherapist. Sometimes to a Twelve-Step support group such as AA. Those of us in the retreat movement increasingly find men who are willing to share their wounds and struggles with other men serious about the spiritual quest. In an atmosphere of trust and sacred space, where confidences are honored, men feel free to disclose some of their secret fears, hurts and failures. There are no judgments or criticism, no patronizing advice. Just the simple message, "We know what you're saying; we've all been there, one way or another." I've always been touched by the line in the Letter of James that says, Confess your sins to one another and pray for one another, that you may be healed" (Jas 5:16). There is great wisdom here. When we share with one another, not necessarily our sins, but our wounds and mistakes, "our cracks and lumps," as I like to call them—we are healed. This is risky business, of course. We fear ridicule and rejection. But most of the time the others will accept us, welcome us, and share with us their own wounded humanity. And we are all stronger for it. This is so different from the adolescent experience, where we bragged about our accomplishments and our exploits (some of them sheer fiction) with a view to feeling superior. But usually we left those encounters feeling both inferior (because there was always someone who could top us) and distant from the group (because competition divides rather than unites).

One other point. When we come to accept our *enosh* condition, we become more accepting and compassionate toward the wounds and struggles of others. In the song "Try to

Remember" from *The Fantastiks*, there's a line that goes: "Deep in December it's nice to remember: without a hurt the heart is hollow." How true. People who haven't suffered wounding or descent, or are in denial about them, are not very helpful companions on the spiritual journey. They tend to be judgmental and analytical, dispensing glib advice and nostrums for our problems. People who have felt their own pain and struggled with life, on the other hand, are usually good to be around. They understand. They're wounded, but they're not snarling or whimpering. They are walking with dignity. As Rabbi Moshe Leib used to say, "No one is as whole as he who has a broken heart."

Such are the positive possibilities of the *enosh* stage of our spiritual journey. We may learn to value the things that really matter and become detached from those that do not. We may become open to a deeper relationship with God, finding inner peace and healing from our compulsions to self-exaltation. And we may experience solidarity and compassion with the rest of wounded humanity, knowing that we truly need one another and are not walking the journey alone.

Six

MATURE MAN: SPIRITUAL INTEGRITY

Males generally are not prepared to be defeated by life. We are culturally conditioned to feel invulnerable, as if we will never be harmed, never lose a job, never get divorced, never develop cancer. Furthermore, our fathers may not have modeled how to deal with hurt and failure, perhaps because they never talked about such feelings in our presence. So, when we ourselves get wounded, we're likely to react with either denial or blame, we may take it out on ourselves (depression, self-pity), or we unload our anger on others (family, society, God).

But we saw that there are positive, redemptive possibilities in our wounding. We can move into a new stage of spiritual growth—chastened, humbled, freed from illusions about what is really important, more compassionate with others, more open to the power of God to heal us. One of the great truths of the Bible is that maturity springs from adversity. "Blessed is the man who perseveres in temptation, for when he has been proved he will receive the crown of life that he promised to those who love him" (Jas 1:12). The Hebrew word for the mature man is 'ish. It is used only to refer to adult males, not to youth or elders. "In other words," Hicks says, "'ish is the mature man, the man who been resurrected from the wounds of life and has a new perspective on the meaning

79

of life and manhood because of that pain" (Hicks 1993, 124). He is a man who knows who he is and what he wants in life.

'Ish as Integration

Psychoanalyst Carl Jung taught that the middle years of life (roughly, ages thirty-five to fifty-five) are the privileged time to befriend and develop the shadow side of our personality—those aspects of the self that we have not attended to in our earlier years. He called this process integration. For mid-life males, one form this takes is the movement toward interiority. Up to this time the man has been investing most of his psychic energy in exterior pursuits: advancing his career, acquiring the symbols of achievement, working on the house, caring for the family. Now, he feels a call to "go inside," to do "soul-work." He finds himself, for example, wanting to nourish his mind. He will start reading more—not just to keep up with his profession but for enjoyment or out of curiosity about other areas of knowledge. He may begin to watch educational programs on television. He may enroll in a class. If he is outgoing and gregarious by temperament, he may begin to relish times of quiet and solitude. If he is the type who keeps moving from one task to another, he may find himself wanting to slow down and be more reflective about his life.

Another way of moving toward interiority is to initiate or renew an interest in the life of the spirit. A good number of men in mid-life have had an awakening or reawakening of spirituality. Often the experience of wounding is the catalyst; the man is compelled to stop and take stock. He has to review his life goals, his priorities, even his assumptions about life. He has to try to figure out the very meaning and purpose of life. In that process he may decide to take a second look at the religious tradition he was brought up in.

Many "baby-boomer" Catholics are at this point in their lives. Often they were given a rather superficial understanding of their faith. Or the teachings and moral values were presented in such a negative light that they found it easy to reject them when they became adults. At mid-life, however, the religious questions resurface: Who is God? Who am I? Why am I on this earth? What is the meaning of life? What is my final destiny? What is the good life? Many people at this point will move from being inactive Catholics to becoming spiritual seekers. Some will find a spiritual home in another church community or another religious movement, but others will try to return to their Catholic roots. Hopefully, they will find a parish community that will welcome them, help them to feel part of the community, and provide them with a mature, adult understanding of Catholicism that will satisfy their mind and lead them toward a personal relationship with God.

There are also men who have never stopped practicing their faith but have kept it in a separate compartment or at the fringe of their consciousness. At mid-life, they may feel a desire for greater integration of their faith with the rest of their life. Perhaps for the first time since high school, they will sign up for a retreat or join their wife to make a Marriage Encounter. They may take up the practice of regular prayer or meditation. Creating time and space to be alone before God, or praying with their wife, many men have found a deep inner peace and connectedness with the ultimate Mystery of the universe.

Dr. Ian Harris, who has surveyed men about spirituality, offers some direct quotations from men about what this inner soul-work has done for them:

I take time to "go within," meditate, reflect. . . . I usually have a basic sense of optimism and faith, that is, a kind of belief in ultimate goodness and a greater purpose of some kind that is beyond human control or comprehension. I think I'm happier because of my spirituality, and better able to cope with stress.

If it wasn't for my spirituality, my faith dimension, I think I probably would have thrown in the towel many years ago. My God has been with me, carved me on the palm of his hand, and has never forsaken me.

It [spirituality] consoles me when I'm hurt. It gives me a place to turn when I have questions. It's a source of joy and hope that my life will continue to grow in health, love, and connection to other people and to mysteries larger than myself.

Integration of the Feminine

Another masculine task of integration is to befriend and nurture our so-called feminine side. According to Jung, we will not be whole persons unless we "make a journey to the other side" of our personality; thus women need to develop some of the masculine qualities to become a more complete person, and men need to do the same with their feminine side. I realize that there is a good deal of controversy about what constitutes masculine and feminine qualities, and I don't wish to get involved in this. My interest is simply this: if we take Jung's categories at face value, what does it mean for a man to integrate his feminine side?

I think it means, for example, moving away from a purely cognitive and intellectual way of viewing reality and paying attention to feelings and emotions, both his own and others'. It means tuning in and becoming comfortable with the fact that sometimes he feels sad as well as happy, bored as well as excited, afraid as well as courageous, irritable as well as peaceful; disappointed as well as satisfied. He recognizes that he does not have to be driven by his feelings, but he does need to be aware of them; otherwise, he will not understand why he acts the way he does. Moreover, he comes to appreciate the positive role of emotions; they are not the enemy of his rational self but rather have the potential to enrich his life with warmth and positive energy. If he is aware of how emotions affect others as well as himself, he will have a deeper basis for understanding and empathy with the people around him. This is often what people mean when they talk about a sensitive male; it is meant as a compliment.

Another sign that a man is integrating his feminine side is

that he is less preoccupied with successes and accomplishments, and more concerned with building and nurturing relationships. People become more important than products. The man begins to treasure his wife, his children, his friends in a deeper way. He may still work very hard at his job, but it is no longer the major determinant of his self-worth or his sense of purpose. He is no longer willing to allow work to interfere with the time and energy he needs to foster healthy relationships. He becomes more transparent and self-revealing in his conversations, takes more initiative in finding out how others are doing, makes it a point to affirm and encourage them in their endeavors. All this comes not from a teeth-gritting sense of duty, but from a deeper place, from the feeling of satisfaction and aliveness that he receives from these simple gestures of love.

Sometimes, however, a man's awakening to relationships can create some tension in his marriage. For example, suppose the wife has spent most of her life caring for the children. Now she is starting to feel her masculine energy and is moving outward to the world of work and achievement. She may not feel inclined to nurturing relationships. So couples at mid-life need to be understanding and patient with one another; they may be at different places in their spiritual journey.

One more indication that a man is integrating feminine energy is growth in the enjoyment and appreciation of beauty. He may start taking an interest in music or art. He may read some of the great literary classics, perhaps even begin writing poetry. None of this ought to be interpreted as losing his masculinity. He is merely continuing a process that is developmentally normal for mid-life. One form this new appreciation of beauty takes is enjoyment of nature. This is present in many men at an earlier age, but it is often repressed because of competing interests and demands. But at mid-life the longing to be connected to the world of nature again makes itself felt. Going hunting or fishing is no longer a test of macho skill or endurance; rather, it is just good to be out in the woods or on the lake. Enjoying the beauty of the golf course is more satisfying than getting the best score. Walking in the park or along the beach, watching the birds, walking in the neighborhood at night after a snowfall—none of these has any functional value, but they are enjoyable for their own sake.

Earlier, I showed how Jesus drew upon his warrior energy to defend himself and others against the criticisms of his opponents. I believe the gospels also reveal Jesus as the mature 'ish male who achieved an admirable integration of masculine and feminine energy. How often do the gospels show him as the first to notice that someone is hurting or in need? For instance, neither the man with the withered hand (Mk 3:1-6) nor the woman with curvature of the spine (Lk 13:10-17) nor the paralyzed man at the pool (Jn 5:1-9) asked Jesus for help. In each case he took the initiative to heal, knowing that his critics would find fault. In the stories of the multiplication of the loaves and fishes, it is Jesus who notices that the people are hungry and enlists the help of the disciples to provide food. He compared himself to a good shepherd, one who knows each of the sheep by name and is willing to risk his life to save any one of them (Jn 10:1-18).

When the disciples were chasing the children away from him, Jesus scolded them and insisted that the children should come to him: "Then he embraced them and blessed them"—a gesture of great tenderness and love (Mk 10:13-16). He was not afraid to show his emotions: he wept over the fate of his beloved city Jerusalem and over the death of his friend Lazarus. Here was a man who, with all his masculine strength, was free to express his gentle, sensitive side without apology.

'Ish as Balance

The Hebrew word 'ish also describes a man who has achieved balance in his life—between work and leisure, solitude and relationships, sacred and secular. According to the Bible, human beings are not to be dominated either by work or by leisure. Rather, they are to reflect God the Creator, who worked for six days and then rested on the seventh. So God gave the Hebrew people a very gentle, sane commandment:

"Remember to keep holy the sabbath day" (Ex 20:8). The purpose of the sabbath rest was twofold: to give people a break from their work, and to remind them of their dignity as God's beloved people. Without this rhythm of work and rest, labor and leisure, our lives would become impoverished. We would easily forget the purpose of our existence. We would lose our spiritual center. We would neglect our most important relationships: God and one another.

Recently I read a brief article by Paraclete Father Liam Hoare entitled "Sabbath: Time Out to Cultivate the Heart." He talks about the sabbath not only as a day of the week, but as a daily, internal practice of the spiritual life. As a society, he writes, most of us live lives of whirlwind activity: "The one with the most who does the most wins. At what cost? So many of the 'winners' report an eventual emptiness and sickness of heart." He recommends developing the habit of an "internal sabbath" that we are prepared to "keep" at any time we need it. He calls it "time out":

- ◆ *Time out to rest:* Since God "rested" on the seventh day, resting is a divine activity, in itself, no reason for shame or guilt. There is great value in taking an occasional "healing interval" during busy times—a short walk; a break for coffee, tea or juice; staring out the window for a while; putting your head back and relaxing the whole body. Resting is an excellent way to keep balance.

- ◆ *Time out to remember:* We need to remember who we are and whose we are. We are beloved sons and daughters of God, formed in the divine image. We need to call to mind the "things that really matter."

- ◆ *Time out to question:* Sabbath time allows us to step back, to ask questions that help us to know the truth of our lives. This can free us from the "cultural trance" that we easily fall into because we're so bombarded with society's lies and half-truths. We need to challenge those attitudes and values that conflict with the gospel of Christ. As Fr. Hoare says, "The reflection that the sabbath provides helps us to question and to disengage from those parts of our lives that are toxic and unhealthy."

Another insight into the importance of balance came to me from a talk I once heard by James Gill, a Jesuit priest-psychiatrist. He works with priests who come into treatment for emotional breakdowns or for sexual misconduct. He asks his clients to diagram how they spent their time just before they were admitted. The diagram usually looked like this:

Then he has them diagram their life at a time they were feeling good and functioning well. It looked like this:

The difference is clear. Life had become unbalanced. Obviously the segments in the second diagram are not all equal—nor should they be—but it is clear that it represents living more holistically. Such a man has a network of supportive relationships; gets physical exercise; nourishes his mind with good reading and cultural interests; and has some relaxing, enjoyable activities to which he can look forward. In the first diagram, life is narrowed almost exclusively to work, and the man became a prime candidate for physical or emotional or spiritual disaster.

I believe the same dynamics are operative for any of us. Being a mature *'ish* male means living a life that is in balance.

Need for a Sense of Mission

A number of times I have spoken of the importance of finding a sense of purpose or meaning for our lives. According to Robert Hicks, this is one of the achievements of the *'ish* man in mid-life. The *gibbor* male, we recall, is full of intense dreams—to win, to be right, to achieve, to be highly regarded. But with wounding, these dreams begin to fade. Hopefully, with the process of reflection and integration taking place in mid-life, a man can begin to dream again. Now, however, his dreams are less tyrannical and compulsive, more realistic and integrated with the larger issues of life. As Daniel Levinson puts it, "It is no longer essential to succeed, no longer catastrophic to fail. He evaluates his success and failure in more complex terms, giving more emphasis to the quality of experience, to the intrinsic value of his work, and their meaning to himself and others" (Levinson 1978, 249).

A book that had a strong impact on me is *Man's Search for Meaning* by psychiatrist Viktor Frankl. He begins with his experience of being a prisoner in a Nazi concentration camp during World War II. As he observed the horrors and indignities inflicted on his fellow prisoners, he noted that many of them became nearly as callous and inhuman as their guards; others simply gave up and died. But some managed to rise above the terrible conditions of their environment. As Frankl says, they were able to find some sense of meaning or purpose there. For some, it was the fact that family members were counting on them to survive. For others, it was to show the Nazis that they could not be broken. Still others were able to find religious meaning in their suffering, linking it with the suffering of Christ for the redemption of the world. After Frankl was freed from prison and went back to his psychiatric practice, he began to see that many of the problems people were bringing to his office were ultimately spiritual problems—questions about the meaning and purpose of their lives. So he developed a new form of treatment that he called logotherapy, by which he tried to help patients examine their lives in terms of their beliefs and values, and to bring their daily decisions into harmony with what they most deeply believed.

We need to know that we have a mission in life. Pastor and spiritual writer Elton Trueblood writes: "Men cannot live well either in poverty or in abundance unless they see some meaning and purpose in life, which alone can be thrilling. Lacking the joy which comes from meaning and purpose, we turn to all kinds of wretched substitutes" (Trueblood 1948, 15). Or, if not "wretched substitutes," at least we tend to settle for an existence which is safe and comfortable, but humdrum. Hicks quotes a bumper sticker that says it all: "Every damn day the same as before." He continues:

> "The saddest men I know are the men who have no real vision for their lives. The man who goes to work every day, comes home, reads the paper, has dinner, watches television, and goes to bed—only to repeat the pattern the next day—is not alive or well. Life has been reduced to mere functioning and maintaining" (Hicks 1993, 132).

The *'ish* male is a man with a mission, a sense of purpose. I find it fascinating that so many businesses, corporations, and even churches have developed "mission statements." The process requires that people sit down together and reflect on what they are all about, what they are trying to accomplish, and what underlying values and principles motivate them. Then they frame these values and goals in language that will be both accurate and appealing. The mission statement is intended to provide everyone in the organization with clear vision and emotional energy for what they are doing. Ideally, everyone—from the CEO to the person who cleans the bathrooms—is clear about the purpose of the organization and feels good about being part of it. Stephen Covey takes the next step: he encourages every individual to develop a personal mission statement, a *personal* philosophy of life. "It focuses on what you want to be (character) and to do (contributions and achievements), and on the values or principles upon which being and doing are based" (Covey 1990, 106).

Whether or not we take the time and discipline to formulate a personal mission statement, I believe the key insight is correct. We need to know that our life on earth is not absurd, not a mere accident of fate, not just an endurance contest in preparation for eternity. We need to know that we have some task to fulfill, some contribution to make, some mission to accomplish. Otherwise, we will be trapped in boredom, cynicism, and never-ending attempts to escape into psychic numbness or mindless pleasure-seeking. I really like what Dr. Bernie Siegel has to say about this in connection with health: "Life is God's gift to us; what we do with it is our gift to God." And Siegel quotes George Bernard Shaw, who said, "This is the true joy in life: being used for a purpose recognized by yourself as a mighty one" (Seigel 1993, 176 and xxi).

Marriage and Family as Mission

The scriptures make it clear that our existence on this earth is not a random occurrence. We have been placed here by God for specific reasons: we are to know and love God; we are to live morally upright lives and thus image the holiness of God; we are to love and care for one another; we are to exercise care and good stewardship for the earth and its resources. That is the "mission statement" for the human family. For most of us, living according to it will take several more specific forms: care for our family; competence in our work; service to the wider community. We will reflect on each of these in a little greater depth.

I realize that not all men will be called to marriage and procreation of children. But for those who are so called, this will be a major form of fulfilling their mission. Unfortunately, the cultural conditioning many men receive does not prepare them well for marriage. In particular, the overemphasis on independence, competition, winning, and being in control makes it difficult for many men to blend their lives with another person. Clayton Barbeau finds that the chief complaint of wives is that their men are not grown-up. This seems to take one of two forms: either the man is a dictator, demanding that everyone conform to his expectations; or he acts like a little boy, avoiding responsibility and demanding that his wife take care of him like a mother (Barbeau 1982).

But the true 'ish man, like many men I have come to know, has risen above the desire to dominate as well as the wish to remain a boy. They are striving, not without some failures, to be responsible husbands. They are sharing with their wives the tasks of maintaining a home, caring for their children, and meeting each other's needs. And they are finding this to be far more satisfying and rewarding than neglect or avoidance of responsibility.

Speaking of meeting each other's needs, one I would like to highlight is the need for affirmation—words and gestures that build up the other's sense of self-worth. It's sad to think how little affirmation people experience in today's world. We hear plenty of criticism for our mistakes and inadequacies but not very much by way of encouragement. If we are doing a good job, we don't expect to be told about it; it's simply what you're "supposed to do."

But I have heard a lot of men speak of a need for affirmation in their lives. I know I need it myself. Being affirmed encourages me to keep giving my best efforts. Without it, I'm tempted to mediocrity and half-heartedness in my ministry. I know I should be more steady, more dedicated to working for the Lord than seeking human recognition, but I have not yet attained that level of purity of heart. Moreover, I know many men who thrive on a little affirmation from their bosses or coworkers. Any good book on management or human relations supports that.

What surprises me, though, is that so many men don't acknowledge that same need in their wives. One of the most frequent complaints I hear from wives is that they receive so little affirmation from their husbands. "While we were dating," they say, "he was so thoughtful and attentive. He would compliment me and let me know he appreciated little things I would do. But now, it seems, he just takes me for granted."

Part of this is natural, of course. Relationships, even intimate ones, tend to fall into routine patterns over time. But couples who do not make the effort to affirm each another over long periods of time are in danger of starving emotionally. Eventually it will mean the death of the relationship. Affirmation, after all, is such a simple action: an offer to help, a surprise note or phone call, a few words like "Thank you for taking care of that," or "I was really proud of you tonight," or "Today at work all the guys were griping about their wives, and I found myself thinking how lucky I am to have you." Small gestures like these cost nothing; but they can go a long way toward strengthening the marriage relationship.

Being a Father

If a man has fathered children, another mission he has been given is to provide them, not just with physical necessities, but with emotional and spiritual care. In the previous chapter I said that one form of wounding men can experience is the absence of a stable and loving father. The contrary is also true: good fathering can be a powerful antidote for the "toxic shame" we talked about earlier.

How do we build children's self-esteem? The answer is so simple: Spend time with them. When I freely choose to spend time with someone, it's a clear sign that I think he or she is worthwhile. One of the problems of our modern era is that fathers don't seem to have time for their children. One study revealed that middle-class fathers interacted with their small children an average of only a few minutes a day. Yet children *need* time and attention from their fathers.

I can imagine how hard it is for a man to come home after working all day at a job that involves talking with adults, often about highly technical matters, and then having to listen to the seemingly trivial chatter of his young children. But dads who neglect this simple gesture will miss precious opportunities to build their children's self-esteem. Charles Francis Adams, a nineteenth-century political figure and diplomat, recorded in his diary: "Went fishing with my son today—a day wasted." On that same day his son, Brook Adams, wrote in his diary: "Went fishing with my father today—the most wonderful day of my life!" We often underestimate the positive power of such simple actions as spending time with someone we love.

I have been a spiritual director to a good number of people. I wish you could hear the tone of voice and see the look of appreciation on the faces of adult men and women as they relate to me how their dads took them for walks and showed them the beauties of nature, or played games with them, or told them stories about "the olden days," or read to them. By contrast, I have also heard many tell me, with great pain, how much they missed all this: "Dad was never around, or if he was, he was always too tired."

Fathers who spend time with their children usually find that it not only builds the child's self-esteem but also provides the father with a deep sense of satisfaction. He discovers that the "trivial chatter" of children gradually becomes more interesting, more inquisitive, more challenging. Fathers have told me that getting involved with their children has kept them young and made them want to continue learning new things. There is a reciprocity, a happy spillover effect, that benefits both father and child.

Sometimes, I think, fathers are too quick to tell their children how different things were "when I was your age." This serves to put distance between parent and child. It would be much more valuable to share with them how *similar* their experiences are. For instance, Dad could talk about how nervous he felt on his first date, or the time he made a great social blunder, or when he was fired from his first job. Then he could add, "But, you know, I learned something important from that. . . ." What a precious lesson that would be for kids. They would get the message that it's okay to be human, to be limited, to have negative feelings and bad days. Numerous day-to-day happenings afford fathers a chance to impart their philosophy of life without preaching or lecturing.

Besides building self-esteem, spending time with children is a simple but effective way to communicate values. Many parents I talk with are deeply concerned about this. In contrast to previous generations, today's children are exposed to value messages from many sources other than their parents. Research shows that young children watch at least thirty hours of television per week. Contrast that with the average few minutes a day that their fathers spend with them. In adolescence, the world of rock music, movies, and the pressures of the peer group have a powerful formative influence. Public schools withdrew from the value arena years ago, leaving a vacuum that will be filled by these other forces. Therefore, parents who cherish their own values will have to make good use of the opportunities they do have to communicate values to their children.

Children need regular exposure to clear value messages. They need to hear parents say things such as, "In this family we expect thus-and-so"; "We don't talk that way in this home"; "We don't believe in that kind of thing"; "This is important to us because we are Christians." It is equally important, however, that parents reinforce the messages by their actual behavior. For example, the most effective way to teach sons respect for women is by the way the father talks about them and by the way he treats them—especially his own wife and daughters.

Work as Mission

It is all too easy for us to view our work or occupation merely as a means to acquire possessions and status or to provide for our families. Or worse, to see it only as a necessary evil or a punishment for original sin. The view expressed in the Bible is much more positive: human labor is participation in the creative activity of God, a task and a mission entrusted to us by God. Even before sin enters the picture, Genesis shows man and woman being given the task of exercising stewardship over the rest of God's creation (Gn 1:28-30). The vocation to work is even more clear in Genesis 2:15, where it states that "the Lord God took the man and settled him in the garden of Eden to cultivate and care for it." In this primitive story of our human origins, the sacred writer is trying to express a profound truth: we humans have been given the responsibility to develop the resources of our earth in creative ways, and to do so with reverence and care.

There is another, even more profound way of putting this truth: God has chosen to make us partners with God in the ongoing mystery of creation. By studying the secrets of nature, by harnessing the powers and energies latent in the universe, we human beings are privileged to cooperate with God's plan "to cultivate and care for the earth." Thereby we glorify God and contribute to the betterment of human life. In that sense, there is truly a sacred dimension to human work. I love to read chapter 38 of the book of Sirach (Ecclesiasticus) in this light. It starts out by praising the work of the physician and the pharmacist, saying that through their healing skills "God's creative work continues without cease" (v. 8). Then it describes the work of farmers, blacksmiths, engravers, designers, and potters, concluding with the beautiful thought that "they maintain God's ancient handiwork, and their concern is for the exercise of their skill" (v. 34). What a positive vision of human labor! Work is not only a means of earning money, it is a vocation. It is a way of developing our potential and sharing in God's creative activity, participating in a mystery greater than ourselves.

Think of the implications of this. When human beings discover cures for disease; when they find healing therapies for mental and emotional distress; when they produce better and safer modes of transportation; when they improve agricultural methods; when they build cleaner and healthier cities; when they find better ways of communicating and processing information; when they equip all citizens with the knowledge and skills they need for meaningful employment—in these and thousands of other ways they are engaging in tasks that are truly sacred. They are fulfilling their mission.

There is yet another facet. If we as human beings are called to perfect the world in accord with the divine plan, then it is crucial that we regard our gifts and abilities as entrusted to us by God. We are not to waste, squander, or misuse them. Rather, we are to develop and use them to the best of our ability. It is true that we never get to use all of our potential. We are limited, and we have to make choices. What saddens me, though, is when I see talented people choosing to live at a level far below their potential. They never read seriously, take a class, watch an educational program on television, or deepen their understanding of their religion. They remind me of the man in the gospel who, out of fear and resentment, went out and buried his master's money instead of working with it (Mt 25:14-30). "Play it safe, don't take chances" is a good way to avoid failure, but it is also a formula for staying only half alive.

Service to Community as Mission

Finally, the biblical *'ish* man is one who has moved beyond self-interest and self-preoccupation. He is not content to withdraw from life and lick his wounds. Rather, his faith in God and in the basic goodness of life releases in him the desire and energy for service to his community. We have seen that the great figures of the Hebrew Scriptures—Jacob, Moses, Elijah,

Amos, Jeremiah—all moved on from their wounding to rededicate themselves to continuing God's work in their community. So it is with contemporary *'ish* men.

The two most common places that men find to serve their communities are the church and civic life. Some men respond to a request from the parish to become involved in one of the church ministries—reader, eucharistic minister, committee member, financial consultant, religion teacher, youth advisor, and others. In doing so, they find a renewed sense of spirituality and of mission. Of course, the same danger lurks here as with any other commitment one makes—the man can become overinvested to the neglect of his primary responsibilities. Once again, the operative word is *balance.*

Other men find themselves drawn toward activities that benefit the civic community. "Wanting to make a difference" drives these men. They volunteer to serve on advisory boards and contribute their expertise in education, management, finances. They help with fund-raising for causes they believe in. They spend many Saturdays supervising youth activities or helping to build or repair homes. If kept in balance, these endeavors do not drain the man or create an undercurrent of resentment. Instead, he finds them life-giving, a welcome change of pace from his regular routine. They give him a sense of contributing to a common good.

Ian Harris's research on men's spirituality turned up a striking statistic: 86 percent of the respondents to his questionnaire said that their spiritual beliefs gave them a sense of mission. Following are some of their actual statements for why they act as they do:

> To leave the world in a better state than I found it, more beautiful and peaceful.
> To share with others the saving gospel of Jesus Christ so that they might come to know Christ personally.
> To help others discover their own spiritual awareness and use it.
> To empower others to create a caring planet.

To help people move out of poverty and to recover
their human dignity.

Robert Hicks offers a fine summary of the *'ish* stage of
male development:

By getting in touch with who we are and doing the necessary reappraisal of our attributes, we are in a better
position to continue our growth more wholistically. The
warrior is in reality a one-dimensional man, focused on
his gun; the phallic male is, of course, over-focused on
his penis; while the wounded male cannot see beyond
his own hurt. Therefore, with the mature man there
begins a new symmetry to life, a new depth and rich-
ness not experienced before" (Hicks 1993, 135).

Truly, these are the men who bless our world with their
presence.

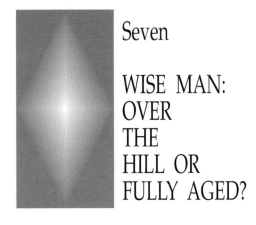

Seven

WISE MAN: OVER THE HILL OR FULLY AGED?

Robert Hicks begins his discussion of the final stage of the masculine journey by contrasting the way two different cultures regard their elderly citizens. First he describes the Middle Eastern "tent fellowship," where the older men gather on soft pillows, drink tea, and discuss the affairs of the day. Anyone from any tribe can come and air his complaints to the elders, as well as ask for advice on any matter. "This rich event," he says, "may appear to us as just 'shooting the breeze,' but it is an interesting mix of social hospitality, business wheeling and dealing, practical counsel, and administrative justice." Here the gray-headed men are regarded as repositories of the wisdom of life. These men are old but not retired. They are involved—leading, modeling, contributing.

By contrast, Hicks says, in contemporary America "our seniors are found huddled in retirement enclaves separated from the mainstream of society and the young. They play golf, bridge, and tennis, watch reruns, and wait for their kids to call"—almost completely cut off from the wider social community (Hicks 1993, 149-51).

Biblical Meaning of *Zaken*

The biblical view of senior citizens reflects the Middle Eastern sense of community involvement rather than isolation.

The sixth Hebrew word for man is *zaken*. The first meaning of the word is "beard," with the connotation of "growing old." It describes the man of mature years with full beard and recognized competence in the community. "This elder," says Hicks, "is far removed from our modern concepts of the retired, uninvolved senior citizen. Instead, his focus is on the social community to which he belongs, either holding office or representing the various groups he values" (Hicks 1993, 152).

Hicks goes on to say that it is tragic to see that so many men burn out or get sick by age forty or fifty. They are in such a hurry to achieve their goal—become a CEO, make the big bucks, have a dream home on the lake, be listed in Who's Who. They fear time is running out and they have not yet "made it." They have uncritically accepted the cultural imperative that says they must achieve at a high level in order to prove their manhood. So they drive themselves to the point that body, emotions, and spirit begin to break.

The scriptures provide us with a much longer and deeper look at the mature years. "The crown of old men *(zaken)* is wide experience," says Ecclesiasticus, "their glory, the fear of the Lord" (Sir 25:16). At the end of his life, Moses wrote a song to teach Israel to remember what God had done for them:

> Think back on the days of old,
> reflect on the years of age upon age.
> Ask your father and he will inform you,
> ask your elders *(zakenim)* and they will tell you
> (Dt 32:7).

That is, when a generation is on the verge of forgetting or denying the power of God to see them through, bring in the elders. They have the knowledge and experience with God to know what really happened, how God works, and how we should trust him today (Hicks 1993, 153). The same conviction is expressed in Psalm 37:25: "Neither in my youth, nor now that I am old *(zaken)*, have I seen a just man forsaken."

At the same time, the scriptures are careful not to claim that age by itself necessarily produces wisdom. Wisdom comes only from an obedient life before God: "I have more discernment than the elders (*zakenim),*" the psalmist says, "because I observe your precepts" (Ps 119:100). And young Elihu tells Job and his companions that "it is a spirit in man, the breath of the Almighty, that gives him understanding" (Job 32:8). So wisdom does not come to a man merely by accumulating years. It requires study of the Scriptures, faith in God, prayer and meditation, and living out the Christian virtues. Apart from these, the elderly life can be empty, bitter, and full of regrets.

Dealing With Unfinished Business

Father Henri Nouwen begins the third chapter of *Creative Ministry* with a troubling story. He describes the visit of a young chaplain intern to a dying man in a hospital. When asked if he wanted to talk, the dying man told the intern in no uncertain terms that the only thing he wanted was to be left alone. "Even a dying animal," he snapped, "can crawl off by itself to die alone. Why am I not allowed the same? You and the others in this place will be respecting my wishes perfectly if you will simply leave me alone" (Nouwen 1971). I remember thinking that I don't want that to happen to me—to die a lonely and bitter man. I think one reason that may happen to people is that they have not dealt with "unfinished business" in their life cycle. So one of the possibilities of the later years is an opportunity to deal constructively with unfinished issues.

Unfulfilled Dreams

Daniel Levinson highlights the role of "the dream" in masculine development. Typically a young man will formulate a dream or vision of what he wants to achieve or accomplish in his lifetime. This is an important dynamic because it gives direction and motivational power to his choices. Whether the dream is to own his own business, keep the family farm, build the nice home in the country, see his children become successful, or travel around the world—his dream is his reason for getting up every morning.

But dreams often remain unrealized, or only partially realized. This is one form of the wounding of life. In Leonard Bernstein's *Mass* there is a scene where the priest holds up a glass chalice full of wine in a gesture of offering to God. Suddenly, he drops it and it shatters on the floor. Then he sings a haunting song, "How Easily Things Get Broken." So too with many of our dreams.

Levinson says that often we will have to modify our dreams or even renounce them entirely. If we have not done this in mid-life, it is a necessary task for *zaken*. Examples of modifying the dream might be: "I never did get to own my own business, but I've had a good job and it was fulfilling." Or, in regard to the children: "Oliver never will move far up the corporate ladder, but he's a wonderful family man." "Sure we were disappointed when Cindy left the convent, but she's so good with those handicapped children, and she's very active in her parish." "We feel bad that our children don't go to church, but they're really Christian in the way they live."

Others have chosen, or been forced, to renounce a dream: "I haven't gained wide recognition as I once hoped I would. But you know, it's not important. I've come to realize other things that matter a whole lot more: family, good friends, a faith to believe in." Someone else will say: "I finally decided to stop trying to live my dreams through my children. I wasn't allowing them to live their own lives."

The fact is, sometimes we have simply bought into the false or shallow standards of the surrounding culture and made them our dream. And now God is calling us to renounce or at least modify that dream. I think this is what Dolores Curran is getting at when she encourages us to stop demanding the perfect marriage and celebrate the fact that we have a "good enough" marriage. The *zaken* is able to extend that concept to other areas: he has a good enough job, a good enough home, a good enough life.

Often in history God's people did not live to see their

dreams fulfilled. Moses died before being able to enter the Promised Land. Jeremiah never did succeed in leading the citizens of Jerusalem to conversion. Zechariah and Elizabeth did not live to see their son, John the Baptist, become the mighty prophet who prepared the way for the coming Messiah. In my own Franciscan tradition there is a remarkable story about St. Francis of Assisi. It took place toward the end of his life. Francis had tried so hard to impart his ideals of voluntary poverty and simplicity of life to his followers. But now, as they were becoming numerous and powerful, he saw them drifting into comfort and pretentiousness. He was grieved in spirit and brought his pain to God in prayer. This is the story:

> One day, noticing and learning that certain ones were giving a bad example in the Order and that the brothers were not maintaining themselves on the heights of their profession, Francis was painfully moved to the depths of his heart and said to the Lord in his prayer, "Lord, I give you back the family you gave me!"
>
> The Lord answered him: "Tell me, why are you so sad when a brother leaves the Order or when others do not walk in the way I have shown you? Tell me, who planted the Order of brothers? Who converts men and urges them to enter it to do penance? Who gives them the strength to persevere? Is it not I? . . .
>
> "That is why I tell you not to be saddened about this. Do what you have to do and do it well. Apply yourself to your work, for I have planted the Order of the brothers in an everlasting charity" (Habig 1973, 86).

God was teaching wisdom to Francis, leading him to become a *zaken*. In his disappointment with the brothers, his self-protective instinct was to withdraw from all involvement with the order. But God reminded Francis that it was God, not Francis, who was in control. Moreover, God pointed out that his dream, although a noble one, would have to be modified in light of the weaknesses of human nature. God's words to Francis can easily be directed to each of us: "Do what you have to do and do it well. Don't betray your own values and convictions, but don't brood or become resentful when others don't follow. Entrust the outcome confidently to my hands."

Painful Memories

Another task we often need to deal with in the senior years is that of letting go of painful memories. We all have a collection of these by the time we reach maturity: family members who hurt or disappointed us, the breakup of a marriage, being fired or cut from a job, being falsely accused, abuse, our own mistakes and failures. If we allow them, memories like these can imprison us in sadness, regret, and bitterness. If left unhealed, we can end up like the tragic man we encountered in the beginning of this chapter.

What is the alternative? Briefly put, we need to make peace with our past. This involves coming to accept, perhaps even embracing, the totality of our unique life cycle, that is, acknowledging that our life has been a blend of joy and sadness, pleasure and pain, health and sickness, success and failure, wounding and healing. We need to see that in the final accounting it was a good life. Erik Erikson calls this final achievement "integrity." He goes on to describe it as "the acceptance of one's own life cycle and of the people who have been significant in it. . . . It thus means a new and different love of one's parents, free of the demand that they should have been different, and an acceptance of the fact that one's life is one's own responsibility" (Erikson 1959).

But what will enable us to move in this direction—from resentment to acceptance? Sometimes it is the realization (which may come only in the reflective times of our senior years) that the painful times somehow turned out for our good. One of my unpleasant memories is of the time I first entered the Capuchin Order at age nineteen. I tried hard to be a good religious, but I was getting more and more tense and stressed-out. Finally, halfway through my novitiate year, the director said I should leave the program. "You may have a vocation to this life," he said, "but you're obviously not ready. Go home and think it over, and maybe you can try again." I was crushed. I felt like a failure. I thought God had betrayed me, or at least let me down.

So I went home and tried to rebuild my life. I got a job, moved out on my own, went to school, began counseling. I needed to develop self-confidence, and the counselor kept pushing me in that direction. Eventually, after eighteen months, I decided to try the order again. This time I made it. But as time went on I could see more clearly how necessary that experience of failure and humiliation had been. The director had been right, of course. Twenty-five years later I was appointed novice director myself. And one of the obvious benefits of my own past experience has been finding it easy to empathize with the struggles of the young men coming into the program.

As I read the scriptures I often find God's servants making peace with their own painful memories. Joseph, for example, was sold into slavery by his envious older brothers. But as time went on, he became the trusted advisor to the pharaoh of Egypt. At the end of the story the brothers, who have now come to Egypt, are afraid that Joseph will take revenge on them. So they beg him for forgiveness. To their relief, Joseph reassures them: "Have no fear. Can I take the place of God? Even though you meant harm to me, God meant it for good, to achieve his present end, the survival of many people. Therefore have no fear. I will provide for you and your children" (Gn 50:19-21). Note Joseph's sense of integrity, to use Erikson's term. Looking back on the wrong done to him earlier, he can now accept it as something that fulfilled the deeper purposes of God and brought about blessings for himself and for many people.

St. Paul expresses the same awareness while he is enduring imprisonment. Writing to the Christian community at Philippi, he says: "I want you to know, brothers, that my situation has turned out rather to advance the gospel, so that my imprisonment has become well known in Christ throughout the whole praetorium and to all the rest, and so that the majority of the brothers, having taken encouragement in the Lord from my imprisonment, dare more than ever to proclaim the word fearlessly" (Phil 1:12-14). So Paul's confinement, while personally painful for him, has paradoxically furthered the cause of Christ rather than hindered it—and that is what really matters for him. He goes on to reflect that even though some are proclaiming Christ from self-serving motives (including envy and rivalry toward Paul), he won't let it bother him. "What difference does it make," he asks, "as long as in every way, whether in pretense or in truth, Christ is being proclaimed? And in that I rejoice. . . . My eager expectation and hope is that I shall not be put to shame in any way. . . " (Phil 1:18-20). Here again is a man of integrity, one who is able to see the larger purposes behind his own sufferings.

I am not saying that painful experiences themselves are good, or that those who inflict injury on us are right in doing so. I'm only saying that *zaken* men have attained a level of wisdom and perspective whereby they can find the positive blessings that have come out of their adversities. There appears to be a renewed interest today in leaving a legacy to the next generation. Daniel Levinson offers some helpful reflections on this notion in *The Seasons of a Man's Life*. At a time when health and nursing costs are depleting the financial resources of many seniors, it is good to know that there are more precious gifts than money that we can pass on to our children. Surely one of these is to share our stories of hardship and the lessons we learned and the gifts we received through painful times.

But what if reflection on our painful memories fails to reveal any positive outcome? What if the experience was a disaster with no redeeming features? Moving toward acceptance then is very difficult, if not dishonest. What is left? One direction that many have found helpful today is prayer for healing. This can be especially appropriate when the memory springs from a traumatic event or series of such events: the early death of a parent; abandonment or rejection by a care-giver; a crippling disease or accident; a disastrous failure; the accidental death or suicide of a loved one; physical or sexual abuse. Prayer for healing can be done either individually or in a group setting. It consists of bringing the painful memory into conscious awareness and then imagining the risen Christ present at the event. This is not mere fantasy. It is based on the Christian belief that Jesus is present to, and Savior of, every event in our life. Then we ask Christ to heal us of the emotional and spiritual wounding we received in those experiences, to free us from the shame, the fear, the anger, the sadness—whatever it is that blocks us from having his peace and love in our heart. Perseverance in this kind of prayer over a period of time often will deliver us from the traumatic effects of painful memories.

The Importance of Forgiveness

Sometimes, when we are praying for healing of past memories, we get in touch with the anger or resentment we still feel toward the person or persons who may have hurt us. Until that block is removed, healing is not possible. And the only way to remove the block, I believe, is to forgive. This is not always easy. The Bible pictures even God having to struggle to forgive a rebellious people (see Hos 11 and Jer 30:12-22). So God understands that forgiveness does not come easily for us.

When the Bible asks believers to forgive injuries, it gives only one reason: we ourselves have received forgiveness from God. The best way to show our gratitude is to pass it on, to extend forgiveness to one another. We should, as St. Paul says so beautifully, "be bearing with one another and forgiving one another, if one has a grievance against another; as the Lord has forgiven you, so must you also do" (Col 3:13). This does not mean that we condone the injury or pretend that it did not hurt. Often it will take some time and arguing with ourselves before we finally are able to reach the point of forgiveness.

Even from a purely psychological standpoint, forgiveness is healthier than its opposite—remaining stuck in resentment. After all, our anger is having no effect on the one it is directed at; we are the only ones in pain. So now there's a double penalty: the original injury plus our ruminating over it. Why not let it go? Question: Must we tell those who hurt us that we forgive them? Sometimes this may be appropriate, but most of the time it is unrealistic. The person may not realize or remember the injury; he or she may even be dead. Forgiveness is basically a deep-down decision of our own will. It takes place in the recesses of our own heart. And usually it is the fruit of prayer.

"Can you ask God to help you forgive that person?" I ask counselees who are struggling with this.

Sometimes they say, "I'm not sure I *want* to forgive."

Then I say, "Well, can you pray to want to?"

"I'm not sure."

"O.K., can you pray to want to want to?"

They laugh, but they get the point: somehow they have to move off dead-center if they are going to find healing. And my consistent experience has been that when people begin to pray with that gut-level honesty, God comes to their aid.

Sometimes the cause of our painful memories is something we ourselves have done or failed to do. Then it is important to remember that what we can do for others we can also do for ourselves. In other words, we can forgive ourselves. Again, some of us may find this difficult.

One reason I will never be a good golfer is that I don't forgive myself for making a bad shot. As a result, my anger at myself throws my concentration off, so I make another bad shot. Likewise, when I think about some of the stupid and sinful things I've done in my own life, those memories stir up shame and guilt. I need to remind myself that God has forgiven me and wants me to be at peace with my past.

What is important is not that we have a perfect track record, but that we have learned valuable lessons from our mistakes and sins. A contemporary Spanish poet puts it so well: "Last night I dreamt: There was a wonderful bee-hive inside my heart. And golden bees were making white combs and sweet honey out of my failures." The wise *zaken* knows that this is the work of God, whose wisdom and power can bring goodness out of our mistakes and failures.

Speaking of God, sometimes our anger is rooted in memories of tragic events or deep disappointments that were the fault of no one; they were caused by fate, bad luck, or whatever. With these we may be inclined to directing our anger at God. This is a normal human reaction that usually subsides with time and reflection. But again, we can get "stuck" here, carrying a low-grade hostility toward God well into the senior years. Like everyone else, I have no clear answer to "why bad things happen to good people," as Rabbi Kushner would say. But a story that comes from the rabbinic literature about the death of Moses may be relevant.

The Bible tells us that when Moses led the people out of Egypt, his human followers (his brother Aaron, his sister Miriam, and the people) all let him down or betrayed him. But he continued to put his trust in God. At the end of the journey, however, it appeared that even God had let him down: God told Moses he would die without entering the Promised Land.

Here the rabbis recount a story. This story is not in the Bible, it comes from the reflections of the Jewish teachers who wrestled with questions such as why life sometimes seems unfair. They say that Moses begged God, saying "I have served you well all these years—please don't let me die." But God replied, "You are a human being, and all humans die." As the story ends, however, God comes down from heaven and takes the soul of Moses—but with a kiss. And at that point, the rabbis say, God wept.

The story tells me that God never promised to spare us from the hurts and tragedies and disappointments of life. Because God has given the priceless gift of freedom to every person, some will choose to use that freedom to inflict injury upon others. As in the Moses story, however, God is not indifferent to our pain. God stands by us and weeps for us. And God is there with healing and comfort, providing the inner strength we need to keep us moving on our spiritual journey. The true *zaken* is able to behold and embrace that mystery in his own life

Realizing New Possibilities

Those who are becoming *zaken* also need to avoid falling into the trap of merely waiting passively for death. Just as the Hebrew elders saw themselves as active participants in the life of their community, so our elders need to resist modern society's attempts to relegate them to the senior citizen enclaves where they live out their days with "their own kind." Instead, they can expect their senior years to be a time of significant contribution. For some, of course, failing health and/or subtle deterioration of mental faculties may influence the type or extent of the role they can play in society in their later years.

Assuming basically good health and mental alertness, however, older men can be invested in life, continuing to utilize their God-given capacities for their own enjoyment and the benefit of the wider society. When I talk with senior men at retreats or in parishes, I often hear how they are involved in volunteer services for the church and civic community. Whether working with the St. Vincent de Paul Society, community meal programs, driving shut-in persons to the doctor, or keeping the financial books for the parish—these men are continuing to experience the sense of mission that we talked about in the last chapter.

In one city there is a program called "Skillbank." It matches people with skills in certain areas (home repair, auto maintenance, sewing, painting, lawn care, etc.) with people who need such services. A good number of retired men make use of their time and skills through this program. Others become involved in one of the intergenerational programs now available in many communities. These provide an opportunity for men to engage in the role of mentor to younger men, who as Hicks says, "need the one-to-one, the life experience, the realism of what life was like for them at the same age.

Without this mentoring, they either 'go it alone' or go it with others who don't know what they are doing" (Hicks 1993, 166-67).

I am always thrilled when I see older people still drinking deeply at the well of life. Most of us, perhaps, have seen lists of people who were still creative and productive in their sunset years. For example:

- ◆ Michaelangelo completed his greatest work at 87,

- ◆ Verdi composed his "Ave Maria" at 85,

- ◆ George Burns won an Academy Award at 80,

- ◆ Albert Schweitzer headed a hospital at 89,

- ◆ Pablo Casals was giving cello concerts at 88,

- ◆ Thomas Edison, Albert Einstein, and Galileo were still making scientific discoveries after 70,

- ◆ Justice Oliver Wendell Holmes set down some of his most brilliant opinions at 90.

A less active, and thus perhaps overlooked area in which *zaken* people can make a major contribution is the witness of their spirituality. I recall the many times I was touched and inspired by my elderly mother's faith and wise spiritual sayings. I often wish there was a forum in our churches where seniors could share with us their hard-won wisdom and their spiritual insights. This does happen at times, for example, in small-group Bible study. I remember an older man named Tom who attended a Lenten series I gave one year in a parish. He was living with inoperable cancer and knew he had only a limited time to live. But he was there every week, and when it came time for audience response and interaction, Tom invariably shared something of his own personal faith that was deeply moving for everyone there. People like this are wonderful models of serenity and peacefulness with the past, even in the face of death. They show us that Christianity really "works." Does Christianity serve to make us more human, more self-accepting, more caring toward others? Does it help us to be less regretful about the past and more confident for the future? Does it bring us some healing for our shame, our fear, our loneliness? Only the faithful *zaken* in our midst can speak to us with authority on these matters.

A final piece of "unfinished business" the elder may need to deal with has to do with the question: Are there still some things I want or need to do before I die? Now that they have the time, many men will act on their desire to travel and see more of the places and people of the world. Others will spend more time getting to know their grandchildren or other family members better. Still others will read and/or take classes in history, archaeology, astronomy, theology—whatever interests them. Yet others will read some of the great literature of the world, attend the theater, do some writing—not to mention correcting the flaws in their golf swing or their bowling form.

Reconciling Relationships

But one of the most important items on the agenda for the senior years, I believe, is the question: Is there any unfinished business in regard to my relationships? There may still be some things seniors need or want to say to people, especially loved ones. Sometimes, when I minister to people at the time of death, one of their deepest regrets is that some person died before they had a chance to say certain things to him or her: "I love you," or, "I want to thank you for everything you have given me." The death of my father and later my mother was difficult for our whole family. But one factor that made both losses bearable was the fact that we took the time to say our good-byes and our "I love you's" and our "thank you's." There was no unfinished business.

Perhaps there are other, equally significant messages we want to leave with our loved ones: "I guess I never told you this before, but I want you to know that

. . . something you said years ago really helped me."

. . . you've been an inspiration to me."

... you were one of the best teachers I ever had."

... I've always been proud of you, and I'm sorry I never told you that before."

It is never too late to communicate these kinds of sentiments to the people we care about. But the sooner the better!

Another form dealing with relationships may take is that of seeking reconciliation. As Hicks writes, "We men can make a mess of our primary relationships during our young and middle-adult years. To make our last years of life satisfying, we should do our best to reconcile any relationships severed or harmed in our earlier years. Good relationships should be nurtured and maintained by whatever means possible" (Hicks 1993, 162). This is simply a corollary of what we stated earlier: For the 'ish male and the zaken male, relationships take on greater importance in life, even as material things and career achievements diminish in importance.

We talked earlier in this chapter about making peace with painful memories by forgiving those who have hurt or disappointed us. But now we shift the shoe to the other foot, asking the further question: Is there anyone from whom I need to ask forgiveness? Two of the twelve steps of AA are directed toward this movement of reconciliation.

Step Eight: "We made a list of all persons we have harmed and become willing to make amends to them all."

Step Nine: "We made direct amends to such people whenever possible, except when to do so would injure them or others."

These are courageous steps. They require a great deal of humility and honesty. It is not easy to admit that we were wrong, that we acted unreasonably and unlovingly—and to ask forgiveness of the other person. But recovering alcoholics will tell you that these steps are absolutely essential. Moreover, when these steps are completed, they feel cleansed and free of the guilt that dogged them for so long.

Our need to seek forgiveness may not be so dramatic, but it is no less important for our spiritual development. There are few human experiences more ennobling than when one person approaches another to say, "I was wrong in what I said or did. I'm sorry, and I ask your forgiveness." Note that this direct approach may not be possible or necessary in all instances. Step Nine states that exceptions can be made when asking pardon and making amends would do more harm than good. But most of the time people will receive such a request gracefully and extend forgiveness readily. Even if they do not, at least we know we have acknowledged our fault. We have acted responsibly.

Seeking reconciliation is one of the great themes of scripture. The story of the prodigal son's return to his father is one that most of us remember. We identify with and are moved by it, because it touches a deep human need. When we mess up, we need to know that we will be given another chance.

In the story of the prodigal son, it is the son who seeks the father's forgiveness. But what if the roles are reversed? What if it is the father, or the *zaken,* who needs forgiveness? We have an example of that in the story of Abraham and Ishmael. When Abraham could not produce a son with Sarah, she persuaded him to do so with her servant Hagar. Abraham and Hagar's son was called Ishmael. But later, when Sarah bore Isaac, she resented the presence of Ishmael and demanded that Abraham drive him and his mother out of the house. Instead of standing up to her, Abraham sent Hagar and her son out into the desert (Gn 21:8-21).

Patrick Arnold comments on this story:

And so Ishmael became a brawler and a raider (Gn 16:12), taking out Abraham's abandonment on everyone else as he ranged across the desert of Paran stalking prey. Abandon a child, and he will always make someone else pay for it. Our society is spawning such desperados like crazy, abandoned by fathers who, for a variety of reasons, can't cope and won't father. Other youths are psychically deserted; though their father may reside in the house and pay the bills on time, he is not spiritually present. Their wild little Ishmaels, desperate to receive authentic father energy, get instead the ersatz masculinity of Dirty Harry, Conan, or Rambo (Arnold 1991, 94-95).

How we wish the scripture story had ended differently—with Abraham going out in search of Ishmael, asking forgiveness for driving him out, being reconciled in a moving father-son embrace. But the Bible shows us Abraham in all his humanness, his cowardice and fickleness, as well as his nobility and steadfast. He is very much like us.

By way of contrast, Robert Hicks tells about John, a man who began drinking in his thirties and lost his wife and children through divorce. For the next twenty years, the wife prevented the children from having any real contact with their father. But then John had a spiritual awakening and discovered the good news of reconciliation. Being reconciled with God was the first step of many in trying to rebuild his past relationships. His adult children are still having a difficult time accepting their changed father, but they are trying. John's sons are allowing him to be a grandfather to their children, and the kids are enjoying his presence in their lives. "He is being a *zaken* in focusing on his primary relationships and trying to reconcile and maintain them" (Hicks 1993, 163-64).

In this final stage of the masculine journey, a man wants to be able to look back upon his life with a sense of satisfaction. To a great extent, I believe, this will depend on whether he has dealt constructively with any previously unfinished business. Has he been willing to renounce or modify the dreams of his youth? Has he reviewed past painful memories, seeing the positive blessings in them and forgiving those (including himself) who caused the pain? Has he continued to invest his energy in personally satisfying pursuits and in activities that benefit his community? Is he maintaining his relationships with people who are significant to him and trying to reconcile with those he might have injured? If so, then he is aging with grace and dignity. He is truly a biblical *zaken*, a wise man. For such a man, death will be the final fulfillment of a meaningful life, a passing over to the fullness of eternal life.

There is no better way to end this chapter than with the words of the wise man Sirach about the *zaken*:

> His care is to seek the Lord, his Maker,
>> to petition the Most High,
>> to open his lips in prayer,
>> to ask pardon for his sins.
> Then, if it pleases the Lord Almighty,
>> he will be filled with the spirit of understanding;
>> he will pour forth his words of wisdom,
>> and in prayer give thanks to the Lord ... .
> Many will praise his understanding;
>> his fame can never be effaced;
>> unfading will be his memory,
>> through all generations his name will live;
>> peoples will speak of his wisdom,
>> and in the assembly sing his praises.
> While he lives he is one out of a thousand,
>> and when he dies his renown will not cease
>> (Sir 39:6,9-11).

Eight

ONGOING SPIRITUAL GROWTH

Chapter One began by asking the question: Is there such a thing as "masculine" (as opposed to "feminine") spirituality? My best answer for a number of years was "I'm not sure." Yet, given my definition of spirituality as "the ongoing endeavor to grow in our relationship with God," it now seems to me that spirituality would be the same for both men and women, at least in regard to its purpose and goal(s): love of God, neighbor, and self; fulfillment of God's plan to perfect creation and bring all people into one human family; final union with God and the human family in the life of eternity. The "ongoing endeavor" to grow toward these goals is the same for both sexes.

On the other hand, it seems to me that men and women will have distinctive ways of approaching and living out their spirituality, though I have not attempted to delineate the differences. I chose instead to use Robert Hicks's schema based on the six Hebrew words for man we have been discussing—trying to view the male spiritual journey as a series of developmental stages. Each stage reflects something about what it means to be masculine at that period of a man's life, though it does not exhaust the totality of what it means to be male or spiritual. But it does alert us to the fact that what characterizes a man in his twenties probably will not characterize him in his forties. The phallic male will have a different set of goals and challenges than will the warrior male—and also with the other stages.

At the same time, we must not imagine that the stages of the journey are sharply defined. They are age-related, but not rigidly so. A man will always be *'adam* (creaturely, noble-but-flawed, subject to death), sexual, wounded. Some of the stages, at least, have to be revisited and reworked as life unfolds. And sometimes a man will get "stuck" in one or the other stage. Overall, however, I think the schema is a useful one, for it describes what ordinarily can be expected at different points in life's journey. When the journey is successful, a man will become less preoccupied with sexual experience, competitive striving, and self-gratification, and more toward mutually enriching relationships, contributions to human betterment, and interior serenity.

Christ as the Model of Manhood

Toward the end of his book, Hicks raises a question that he often hears at the retreats he conducts: "Where does Jesus fit into all this?" He answers that Jesus "fits very nicely" in the sense that he serves as a role model for journeying through the six stages. Scripture says: "Therefore, since we have a great high priest who has passed through the heavens, Jesus, the Son of God, let us hold fast to our confession. For we do not have a high priest who is unable to sympathize with our weaknesses, but one who has similarly been tested in every way, yet without sin" (Heb 4:14-15). Another scripture refers to Jesus as "the second Adam" (1 Cor 15:47), indicating that Jesus shared our humanity completely. He was truly *'adam*—like us. Therefore, he can completely empathize with us on our journey.

It helps us immensely to remember that Jesus experienced the full range of human physical and emotional life. He knew hunger and thirst and weariness. He and his parents were refugees and immigrants in a foreign country (Egypt). He experienced opposition and rejection from those he was trying to help. He was often misunderstood, even by his own disciples. He felt the hurt of betrayal by a friend and the terror of impending death. The above passage even affirms that he "was tempted in every way that we are." If we are to take that seriously, we have to include sexual temptation. Jesus was also *zakar*, a sexual male. But though tempted, he did not sin. That is the difference between Christ and ourselves. Yet that fact does not separate him from us. Jesus shared the experience of being tested—as we are—in every stage of the male journey.

As *gibbor*, Jesus had to draw upon his warrior energy on numerous occasions. "He warred for the truth," Hicks writes, "for the true meaning of the Law and its application, for compassion, for justice, for the sake of his Father's will. If we need a spiritual warrior as a model, then we see it perfectly in the life of Christ" (Hicks 1993, 181).

Jesus also shared in the wounding of the *enosh* male. His passion and death are the most dramatic examples, but perhaps he is even more like us in his experiences of failure.

One day, after Jesus had worked so many signs and wonders for the healing of people, "the Pharisees came forward and began to argue with him, seeking from him a sign from heaven to test him. He sighed from the depth of his spirit and said, 'Why does this generation seek a sign?'" (Mk 8:11-12). We can almost hear the weariness and exasperation in Jesus' voice as he seems to say, "What more can I do to convince you?"

Another time Jesus admonished the disciples, "Watch out, guard against the leaven of the Pharisees and the leaven of Herod." They thought he was upset with them because they forgot to bring bread along in the boat, but Jesus was really talking about inner attitudes, the "yeast" of the Pharisees (hypocrisy) and the "yeast" of Herod (worldly ambition). He reminded them that he had been able to feed hungry crowds by multiplying bread, but that it is much harder to enlighten minds and convert hearts, including their own. His parting words, spoken with sadness and disappointment were, "Do you still not understand?" (Mk 8:14-21).

One day Jesus was teaching the crowds about the

eucharist, telling them they would need to eat and drink of his body and blood if they wanted to have spiritual life. Many of his listeners were disturbed. "As a result of this," the Bible says, "many [of] his disciples returned to their former way of life and no longer accompanied him" (Jn 6:60-66). That must have been a major wounding for Jesus.

Even at the Last Supper, according to Luke, the twelve apostles were still bickering over which of them was the greatest. We can almost hear the pain in the Lord's voice as he says, in effect, "Fellows, you still don't get it, do you? The one who is truly great is the one who serves the rest" (cf. Lk 22:24-27).

It is not difficult to see the adult Jesus as the embodiment of the biblical ideal of *'ish*, the fully mature man of integrity. This is revealed most clearly after Christ's resurrection from the dead, when we see him reconnecting with his disciples and encouraging them in their time of disillusionment (Lk 24:13-49). Above all, he is focused on mission. In one sense his own mission is completed: "[Father] I glorified you on earth by accomplishing the work [his preaching, passion and death] that you gave me to do" (Jn 17:4).

At the same time, he is now concerned with forming and empowering the disciples (mentoring them) so they can continue his mission till the end of time. Then, just before his ascension into heaven, he formally commissions them: "Go, therefore, and make disciples of all nations ... teaching them to observe all that I have commanded you. And behold, I am with you always, until the end of the age" (Mt 28:19-20).

The gospels also show Jesus as the ideal *zaken*. Though he lived barely into his thirties, he was wise beyond his years. Already at the age of twelve, he was found in the temple "sitting in the midst of the teachers, listening to them and asking them questions, and all who heard him were astounded at his understanding and his answers" (Lk 2:46-47). When he began his teaching mission, we read repeatedly that the crowds were "astonished at his teaching, for he taught them as one having authority" (Mt 7:28; Mk 1:22; Lk 4:32). While teaching in his hometown of Nazareth the townsfolk remarked, "Where did this man get all this? What kind of wisdom has been given him?" (Mk 6:2). Toward the end of his life, the chief priests sent some deputies out to arrest Jesus. When they came back empty-handed, the priests demanded to know why they had not brought him in. They replied, "Never before has anyone spoken like this one" (Jn 7:46). Even those who were ill-disposed toward Jesus found themselves struck by the force of his wisdom. Moreover, we see Jesus, the *zaken*, eager to leave the rich legacy of his teaching and example to those who would believe in him. And he went to his death with no unfinished business. He entrusted his mother to his beloved disciple (Jn 19:26-27), and he even tried to convey his forgiveness to his betrayer, Judas, calling him "my friend" (Mt 26:50).

When we contemplate the life of Christ in this way, we can see how profoundly he embodied the six qualities of manhood that we have been studying. As Hicks says, "Jesus is the voice we need at every stage on the male journey to help pull us out of our caves and get us moving forward on our journeys. He has always been before us, no matter where we are. He can be trusted as our guide" (Hicks 1993, 182-83). I would add that Jesus is not only our guide, but also the source of our strength. A guide is not of much help if we are too weak or weary to follow. Jesus' power ("grace") is available to us to sustain us on the spiritual journey. We are not walking merely under our own power.

At the same time, we need to do our part. Catholic theology has always seen spiritual growth as an interactive process: human effort accompanied by divine grace. What does that "human effort" involve? How do we continue the spiritual journey?

A few years ago I gave a talk at a men's retreat entitled "A Six-Step Program for Spiritual Growth." I based it on the twelve steps of AA, and I jokingly told the fellows that my program was only half as difficult. What I'd like to offer now is a revised version of that six-step program with some of the insights of Promise Keepers incorporated. I don't know a lot about that movement, but I like the key concept: one reason our society is in such a chaotic state is that so many men are promise *breakers*. What could happen if Christian men would commit themselves to becoming promise *keepers*—to honor Jesus Christ through prayer and worship; to form supportive relationships with other men; to practice moral and ethical purity; to build strong marriages and families; to support the mission of the local church; to reach beyond racial and denominational barriers; and to influence the world through the power of the gospel?

The six steps below are not so much a program as a process. I think of a program as something that has a beginning and an end; a process is ongoing. Moreover, these six steps are not once-and-for-all events. We need to engage them repeatedly over our life cycle. They cut across and through all the developmental stages we outlined in the previous chapters. The classical word for what we are about to describe is conversion. For Catholic Christians (unlike some fundamentalist Christians), conversion is not a single, life-changing event, but an ongoing process. St. Paul speaks about how important it is to "grow to the full maturity of Christ" (Eph 4:15). So we have to work through the six steps many times in our journey toward wholeness.

Step One: Recognizing Our Need to Change

The first of the six steps: "We admit that we are troubled in spirit, dissatisfied with the quality of our lives." The first step in any movement toward change is a sense of restlessness and dissatisfaction with the way our life is going. People do not change unless they want to. But what creates the want? Most of the time it is not argument, persuasion, or even threat of punishment—at least not when it comes to spiritual conversion. I consistently have found that people are ready for change only when they experience a significant degree of internal restlessness or dissatisfaction. It may be perceived only vaguely, but there is a sense of discomfort that cannot be ignored.

Usually the discomfort has been simmering for a long

time before it breaks fully into consciousness. Sometimes the catalyst will be an experience of loss: a job terminated, a romance or friendship turned sour, a failed project or program. One Vietnam veteran drifted around for several years after the war. He told me he realized he needed God the day he found himself flipping a coin to decide whether he should head for Michigan or California.

But often the dissatisfaction is more subtle: a critical remark from our wife, child, or friend that hits home; a movie character we react to by saying "That's me!"; or hearing or reading about someone who embodies ideals we once had but have somehow lost sight of. (I would venture to say that the very fact you are reading this book indicates that you are looking for something more in life.)

The experience of dissatisfaction need not always arise from something negative. Some men, like Francis of Assisi, find it in the midst of success or enjoyment. One day, they find themselves asking: "Is that all there is? Is this really what life is all about?" Whatever the cause of our discomfort, it is when we acknowledge it that we are ready for the next step.

Step Two: Seeing a New Vision

The second step: "We come to see a new and better vision of what our life could be."

What do men do with their feelings of restlessness and dissatisfaction? Some deny, repress, or otherwise try to muffle them. Others, not knowing what else to do, simply endure them. For the spiritual process to continue, however, some alternative possibility must open up, some new vision. We become aware that there must be a better way.

A new vision can come to restless seekers from practically any source: reading the scriptures, hearing a homily, watching a movie, listening to a song, having a conversation with a friend. Somehow we feel touched by God. It is what theologians call a graced moment. There is a clear realization that there is indeed something more.

The New Catholics is full of stories revealing this second step of the change process. James Thompson, for example, after describing how his life was careening out of control, says he found his first glimpse of hope through reading the novels of Graham Greene. For the first time in his life, he understood the meaning of the cross: "Jesus Christ had died for even the most forlorn of sinners." For Dale Vree it was the example of dedicated Christian friends he encountered in East Berlin. For Peter Weiskel it was likewise the example of a Christian family who, he says, "fully embodied both duty and delight. I thought one had to choose for one or the other, and be either a dutiful Christian or a happy, irresponsible pagan" (O'Neill 1987).

This second step presumes, however, that we are actively seeking, or at least are open to, a new awareness. Recall what we said before about the interaction between God's grace and our own efforts in spiritual growth. We need to be looking, listening, reading, and praying. Like the blind man in the gospel, when Jesus asks what we want of him, we respond that we want to see (cf. Lk 18:41). This is our prayer for spiritual vision.

Step Three: Deciding to Change

The third step in the process: "We make a conscious decision to change our thinking and our behavior in accord with our new vision."

It is of no value to see a new possibility but do nothing to actualize it. This step is the tough one, because there is something deep in human nature that resists change. As the saying goes, The devil you know is better than the one you don't know. We may not be satisfied with how we are doing right now, but at least it's familiar. If we make a change, we may end up feeling even worse. At the very least, we may balk at the price we have to pay in order to follow our new vision. So we seldom make a clean and instantaneous break with our habitual patterns of thinking and acting. Rather, we go through some period of struggle and resistance. It is at this point that we may decide that the price is too high and settle back into our former patterns. Or we may persevere in our desire to move forward.

The third step is first of all a conscious decision. It is not something we slide into halfheartedly like most New Year's resolutions. Fully aware of the cost of change, and also of the unsatisfying consequences of staying in our rut, we deliberately opt for change. Usually the change involves both thought and action. Alcoholics understand that their problems are rooted in what they call "stinkin' thinkin'." They've learned a set of self-deceptive and self-destructive ways of thinking that set them up for the next bout of drinking: "I'm under a lot of stress, and I need a couple of drinks to relax"; or "Everyone else here is drinking and having a good time— why shouldn't I?" A great deal of the recovery process involves learning to challenge these ways of thinking and to replace them with thought patterns that are conducive to health and sobriety.

For those seeking spiritual growth, this process is crucial. The gospel of Christ is in constant tension with our cultural gospel, which says that the "good life" consists in possessing, consuming, enjoying, and winning. What's wrong with this picture? Nothing—except that these goals can become all-consuming. They become addictive, driving us relentlessly until our lives are out of balance. And in the end they disappoint us. Often without even realizing it, we absorb the cultural gospel almost by osmosis. We grow up with our own forms of "stinkin' thinkin'":

- You're nothing if you don't have. . . .

- Everyone else is cheating, so. . . .

- You work hard, you deserve. . . .

- Why try hard to be responsible? Nobody else is. . . .

- It's not your problem if some people are hungry or homeless; you've got troubles of your own. . . .

When we come to see a new vision, we are challenged to examine these more-or-less conscious assumptions and to either discard or revise them.

But ridding ourselves of "stinkin' thinkin'" is not sufficient. The third step asks that we also revise our behavior in
conformity with our new vision. So we make conscious decisions: to listen more respectfully before we spout off our own
opinions; to be more attentive to our wife when she needs to
talk; to spend more quality time with our children; to challenge some company practice that is harmful to people or to
the environment; to volunteer some of our time to help with a
project at church or in the community; to stop being negative
and critical about something that cannot be changed.
Sometimes the decisions may seem relatively minor, other
times they may be major breakthroughs. In a way, it doesn't
really matter. The decision will make a difference in the long
haul of our spiritual journey.

I find a connection between this third step and some of
the statements of Promise Keepers. Their third promise is: "A
Promise Keeper is committed to practicing spiritual, moral,
ethical, and sexual purity." The intent is crystal clear. Promise
Keepers are men who have surveyed the moral landscape of
our culture and found it to be a wasteland. They are determined to improve it by the consistent practice of purity—
which I take to mean moral integrity in accord with the Ten
Commandments and the gospel law of love. The only nuance
I would add is that this is not a one-time commitment but
rather a whole series of decisions occurring throughout the life
cycle.

The fourth promise is: "A Promise Keeper is committed
to building strong marriages and families through love, protection, and biblical values." Again, it is not difficult to see the
need and the basis for this promise. These men have seen the
wreckage in so many families because men have failed to
invest themselves in building a strong marriage and family
life. Too often they have withdrawn, emotionally if not physically, from the home scene. So Promise Keepers want to rectify
that defect.

While we cannot help but applaud this direction, we
need to be clear about what we mean by "biblical values."

Sometimes I get the impression that the Promise Keepers program favors a model of marriage and family that locates authority and decision-making in the husband/father. Although at first glance it appears that scripture favors this view of the husband/father as head of the family—St. Paul says clearly, "Wives should be subordinate to their husbands as to the Lord" (Eph 5:22)—a closer reading of the whole section leads us to a more complete interpretation. The key is in the verse just before, where Paul is talking to the whole Christian community and says, "Be subordinate to one another out of reverence for Christ" (Eph 5:21). Jesus himself often warned the apostles not to exercise power and domination over others: "For the Son of Man did not come to be served but to serve and to give his life as a ransom for many" (Mk 10:45). Paul is reminding Christians that they must not get bogged down in power struggles among themselves. If everyone keeps demanding his or her own way, nothing will get done; the reign of God will be held back rather than built up. The body of Christ will suffer from internal divisions. The remedy, Paul says, is to defer to one another; that is, to be willing to sacrifice some of our wants and preferences for the sake of unity in the body of Christ.

In the verses that follow Paul simply applies this principle to Christian marriage. Wives and husbands must learn to defer to one another out of reverence for Christ, out of regard for the covenant, the sacramental bond in Christ that is the heart of marriage. When Paul says, "Wives should be subordinate to their husbands as to the Lord," he is saying, "They should be willing at times to sacrifice some of their will, their freedom, for the sake of strengthening the marriage relationship." And he implies that this deference is to be mutual when he adds, "Husbands, love your wives, even as Christ loved the church and handed himself over for her" (v. 25). That is, "Be willing at times to sacrifice some of your own comfort, will, or interests for the sake of strengthening the marriage bond."

This is a profound view of marriage, because it sees

Christ as the center. It is he who has authority, even over the individual wills of the partners. This view is strongly counter-cultural, especially in an age when the culture exalts individuality and personal autonomy. The Christian vision calls for a willingness to yield some of that individuality and autonomy for the sake of building the marriage relationship. It calls for husbands and wives to form a new kind of partnership. While reverencing each other's uniqueness and freedom, they are to blend their lives in a deeper unity in Jesus Christ, always putting him at the center of their relationship and asking, "What is the Lord asking of us? What is the loving way to act in this situation?"

I have dwelt at some length on this third step of the conversion process because I think it is the most crucial step. Unless and until we begin making concrete decisions to improve our ways of thinking and acting, spirituality will always remain something trapped in our head. We may think good thoughts and talk a good line, but it doesn't make any significant impact on the way we live. On the other hand, if we are serious about spiritual decision-making, the next three steps will seem logical and natural, if not necessarily easy.

Step Four: Ongoing Self-Examination

The fourth step can be expressed this way: "We engage in continuous personal inventory, striving to correct negative habits and to replace them with positive ones."

In a sense this step is a simple extension of the first three. It calls us to an ongoing process of interior reflection whereby we get in touch with our dissatisfaction, perceive a new vision, and make decisions for change. In my experience, however, this is a discipline that does not come easily. We are busy with our jobs, our families, our projects, our entertainments. We do not ordinarily take the time to reflect on what is going on inside our souls. As a result, we tend to live on the surface rather than out of our depths. Socrates pointed out the price we pay for superficiality when he said, "The unexamined life is not worth living."

In our own time, Stephen Covey reminds us of an endowment we possess that differentiates us from the animals: self-awareness. This ability, Covey says, "is the reason why man has dominion over all things in the world and why he can make significant advances from generation to generation. . . . This is also why we can make and break our habits" (Covey 1990, 66). He urges his readers to develop the habit of self-reflection on their daily experiences. This will have a number of positive payoffs: It will greatly expand our self-awareness, thereby freeing us from unrecognized assumptions and compulsions which can drive us into unhealthy decisions; it will help us to recognize when we are acting out of our own values or merely out of cultural expectations or the need to please others; and it will enable us to correct habits that are dysfunctional.

Recovering alcoholics have long recognized the value of regular self-examination. Step Four asks them to make "a searching and fearless moral inventory" of themselves. This is usually a one-time experience that requires hours of honest self-scrutiny. But Step Ten commits them to continuous personal inventory and to admitting honestly when they have been wrong in their thinking or acting. It is the only way for them to avoid relapsing into the patterns that led them down the path of sickness and addiction.

I do believe that we need to spend some time each day in self-reflection. But whereas AA appears to emphasize faults and negative behaviors, I believe our examination should include both positive and negative dimensions. I take some time in the morning, as part of my prayer, to review the events of the previous day. When I see that I acted responsibly and lovingly, I thank God and let myself experience the good feeling that comes from this. And when I see that I acted stupidly, selfishly, or unlovingly, I try to understand why, what was driving me, how I went off course, how my thinking was impaired. Then I ask God to help me learn something from this experience and to handle a similar situation better the

next time. I have become convinced of the need for this kind of self-monitoring if we are to continue to grow spiritually. It is sometimes said that we become what we welcome. An older admonition was to avoid occasions of sin. That is, if we place ourselves with people or in situations that pull us toward negative behavior, or if we welcome into our consciousness ideas and images that are ungodly, we will become negative and ungodly ourselves. Dag Hammarskjold, former secretary-general of the United Nations, had a vivid way of putting it:

> You cannot play with the animal in you without becoming wholly animal, play with falsehood without forfeiting your right to truth, play with cruelty without losing your sensitivity of mind. He who wants to keep his garden tidy doesn't reserve a plot for weeds (quoted in Covey, 305).

By the same token, if we welcome positive persons and thoughts into our awareness, we become more positive and life-giving persons ourselves.

This leads me to say a few words about what Catholics call the sacrament of reconciliation. I believe that Christ gave us this sacrament out of his deep understanding of human nature. Most of us need to tell our failings to another human being in order to feel "cleansed" and forgiven. The Fifth Step of AA is founded on this psychology: "We admitted to God, to ourselves, and to another human being the exact nature of our wrongs." Generations of bartenders and psychotherapists can testify to this human need. However, while anyone may be able to "hear our confession," no human being can give assurance of forgiveness. At most our human listener can say, "I understand your behavior and I accept you in your humanness. I can even give you a 'penance' in the form of a fee. But if you want assurance that you are forgiven by God, I suggest you go to your priest or minister."

Even though we may not have serious sins to confess, it is good for our spiritual growth to bring ourselves to the sacrament of reconciliation several times a year. This helps us to remain honest and humble about who we are. We are not flawless supermen; we are fragile, forgetful, self-serving human beings. Yet at the same time, we are the redeemed, baptized, beloved sons of a Father who is always ready to pour out his love and mercy upon us. Reconciliation helps us recognize and maintain our true identity.

Today I hope we are beyond trying to enumerate each and every one of our sins, or the routine laundry list: "I forgot my meal prayers; I cursed and swore; I had bad thoughts. . . ." It is far more helpful to bring before the Lord some of the basic attitudes or patterns that block our spiritual growth. For instance, "Father, I see in myself a streak of laziness. It shows up in the fact that I keep putting off chores my wife asks me to do. Or I get irritated with my kids when they want a little attention and interest from me." Or, "I'm seeing a pattern in myself of always needing to be right. I react with anger when someone, especially someone in my family, questions one of my ideas or actions." As I sometimes tell retreatants, "If you don't know what your sinful attitudes are, ask your wife or your kids!" When we bring these tendencies before Christ in the sacrament of reconciliation, he is able to touch them with his healing power and gradually to free us from their dominance.

Step Five: Regular Prayer and Meditation

This step I have taken practically verbatim from the Eleventh Step of AA. My version: "We seek, through prayer and meditation, to improve our conscious contact with God, praying for knowledge of his will and the power to carry it out."

The heart of spirituality is our relationship with God. Whatever programs or practices we might utilize are helpful only insofar as they foster growth in that relationship. But undoubtedly one of the essential practices in the spiritual life is prayer. Why? Because relationships grow only through communication. If you tell your wife you want to deepen your relationship with her but never bother to talk or listen to her, you would soon hear some unflattering remarks about your credibility, and rightly so.

Prayer is basically a form of communication. I like to define prayer as "any act whereby we consciously attend to the presence of God within or around us." The two key notions here are "presence of God" and "consciously attend." God is continually inviting us into relationship. That is the first movement of spirituality. The second movement is our response to God's invitations. When we consciously attend to the presence of God, we are responding. We are completing the circle. We are praying. Our prayer can take a variety of forms. We may use a formula prayer, such as the Our Father or one of the psalms. But we may also just talk to God in our own words, or sing a song, or quietly reflect on some word or truth that has struck us in a new way. We may simply remain in silent wonder at the Mystery that surrounds us. All these are valid forms of prayer. We can be as free and open with God as we are with any other friend. We don't have to pretty up our words or put on a good front. If we're heavy with discourage-ment, smoldering with resentment, feeling lustful, suffering loneliness, wanting revenge—we can bring it all to prayer. God knows it all anyway. As the scripture says, "No creature is concealed from him, but everything is naked and exposed" to his eyes (Heb 4:13). But this divine knowledge is healing, not intimidating. The author continues: "So let us confidently approach the throne of grace to receive mercy and to find grace for timely help" (Heb 4:16).

I tend to use the words "prayer" and "meditation" inter-changeably, though technically they are distinct. We can med-itate for the purpose of reducing stress, without any explicit reference to God. We just relax our body and focus our mind on some word or mental image. To turn this practice into prayer, all we need do is use a word or image that connects us with God (or Jesus, or the Holy Spirit). Meditation is also used to describe the practice of reading a brief passage from Scripture or some other source and then reflecting on it, trying to connect it with our own life, talking to the Lord about it. Numerous books of short meditations are available. One that intrigues me is *Meditations for Men Who Do Too Much.*

Regular prayer, incidentally, is the very first commitment of Promise Keepers: "A Promise Keeper is committed to honoring Jesus Christ through worship, prayer, and obedience to his Word."

I cannot leave this section on prayer without speaking about that other great Christian sacrament: the eucharist. Catholics have always been taught that the liturgy of the eucharist, the Mass, is the highest form of prayer. One of the problems, however, is that too many Catholics still attend Sunday Mass only out of a sense of obligation. They expect little and receive little. But there are many others who attend with at least a vague hope that they will be touched, uplifted, and find a bit of courage to help them through another week. These are the people I want to speak to here.

I once read a marvelous booklet by Father Eugene Walsh entitled *The Ministry of the Celebrating Community.* It left a deep impression on me and gave me some helpful ideas on how to be a better presider at the eucharist. But Walsh was really writing for the whole congregation assembled at Mass. He began by asking: What do we hope will happen at the liturgy? What is the real purpose of our gathering? His answer: to create for everyone there the possibility of an experience of God. That really struck me. Not a word about obligation or mortal sin. No, we come to the Mass for a profoundly positive reason: to experience the presence of God, to "taste and see how good the Lord is" (Ps 34:9). That brings us back to our definition of spirituality as "the ongoing endeavor to grow in our relationship with God."

Father Walsh reminds us that there are two natural and strong driving forces always at work between God and ourselves: first, the fact that God is always reaching out and inviting us to share in his love; and second, each of us at some level is desperately searching for fulfillment in life. The purpose of liturgy, then, is to recognize and celebrate the presence of God giving hope and meaning to our lives. We do that not just by ourselves, but in union with Christ and with our brothers and sisters gathered around the Lord's table.

If our presence at Mass is to have any spiritual impact, however, we need to "pay attention" (the central act of prayer) to what is going on around us and within us. How is God being revealed? What does God want us to see or hear? How are we being encouraged, strengthened, nourished? How are we being challenged? Can we see that disagreeable fellow at work in a new light? Can we surrender our anxieties to the Lord this week? As we approach the moment of communion, what are we hoping to receive from Christ? Can we let our outstretched hand or tongue symbolize our profound need for Jesus in our life? Catholics have always believed that the eucharist is the privileged place of our meeting with God. We need to claim that heritage and make it real for ourselves.

Step Six: Reaching Out to Others

The sixth and final step in the process of spiritual growth is: "Having had our own spiritual awakening, we try to share with others what we have found."

This is modeled on the twelfth step of AA. Alcoholics have found that one of the best aids to their recovery is to reach out to other addicts with the good news that sobriety and healthy living are possible also for them. Moreover, they've found that recovering addicts are in the best position to reach out to and help other addicts, because they are familiar with the pain as well as all the mechanisms of denial and resistance likely to be put up by the addicted.

The first five steps are aimed more or less at our own internal conversion and spiritual nurturing. The intent in this step is to develop a sense of mission, of action for the sake of helping other people and improving our social environment. Earlier we saw that this is one of the characteristics of the mature man, the *'ish* male. This step is more inclusive than AA's; we reach out not only to those whose lives are out of control, but to those many others who are spiritually searching. Our efforts may be focused within the church and directed to the wider world.

Let's look at service in the church first. Promise Keepers puts it this way: "A Promise Keeper is committed to supporting the mission of the church by honoring and praying for his pastor and by actively giving of his time and resources." One of the aspects of Promise Keepers that I like is the fact that it does not draw men away from their local church into a separate or elitist group; it anchors them firmly in their congregation and links them to their pastor. I don't think "honoring" the pastor implies that we have to agree with every one of his opinions or directions. If we have honest disagreements we can try to resolve them in a spirit of charity and dialogue. And "actively giving of time and resources" translates easily into the concept of stewardship.

Catholic laity today are becoming more aware that the church needs their gifts and their services. Certainly one reason for this awareness is the dramatic decrease in the number of priests and religious which is leaving large gaps in the church's ministry and outreach. Necessity sometimes leads us to the rediscovery of some forgotten or neglected truth; in this case, it has served to remind us that ministry and service are the vocation of the entire church, not just the bishops, priests, and religious. The early church took this for granted. In fact, St. Paul reminded the Roman and Corinthian believers that each of them had some gift or talent that could help build up the entire community in Christ (see Rom 12:3-8; 1 Cor 12:4-11).

This is the biblical and theological background for what we see happening in the church today: men being ordained as permanent deacons, men and women being trained as lectors, eucharistic ministers, and catechists. Some of the men I have met are finding a great deal of fulfillment in the exercise of these ministries. They don't just get up and read the scriptures at Mass haphazardly; they pray over the word of God ahead of time, digest it personally, and then proclaim it with power and conviction. When they minister the consecrated bread and wine, it is evident that they believe they are inviting communicants to share in the body and blood of Jesus Christ. When they bring the eucharist to the sick or shut-ins, they listen to and pray with them, and they bring something of the parish's care and concern into their life. I marvel at how some catechists keep giving their best, week after week, sometimes to a group of unresponsive kids, because they are so convinced of the truths of the faith.

But these are not the only forms of ministry. I have dealt with a lot of men who are involved in their parish councils or commissions. They know they have something positive to contribute, even when it is not always appreciated. Some men and their wives assist the pastor in preparing engaged couples for marriage. Today no pastor or pastoral team can expect to have expertise in every area that affects parish life and certainly can't expect to do everything without help. The support of the laity is absolutely indispensable.

Apart from these more visible ministries, there are a great number of men whose service is more hidden: ushers, those who set up tables and chairs for parish functions, men who get involved with the youth of the parish, helping on retreats, camping trips, athletic events. Moreover, I believe there are gifts that we haven't even begun to tap. For example, we often hear that bartenders listen to more problems than most priests and psychiatrists. Why couldn't we train lay people in "the art of Christian listening" and let them be available for people who need to talk to someone in a context of faith?

This sixth step, the mission step of spiritual growth, must not be seen as limited to "churchy" activities. It is even more urgent to direct our vision and our activities toward the wider arena of the secular world, for that is where most people live out their lives. The final commitment of Promise Keepers says, "A Promise Keeper is committed to influencing his world, being obedient to the Great Commandment (love of God and neighbor) and the Great Commission (bringing the gospel of Christ to others)." Earlier we talked about some ways that men influence the world by giving a good example, by making responsible decisions on their jobs, and by being involved in community programs to improve the quality of human life. They are being obedient to the Great Commandment of love.

But I am also edified by the sixth commitment of Promise Keepers reaching beyond racial and denominational barriers to demonstrate the power of biblical unity. Men are encouraged to meet and talk with at least one man of a different race or denomination each month. At a time when so many of us are divided from one another by fear and prejudice, this is a bold and courageous attempt to forge unity.

A personal experience brought this principle home to me in an unforgettable way. One Saturday evening I was driving home after Mass. As I left the freeway and stopped for a traffic light, my engine died. It was overheated and wouldn't restart. I was in a high-crime section of Detroit, and I was apprehensive. Just as I got out of the car to get help at a service station, a black man pulled up behind me. He got out of his car and asked if he could help. He quickly diagnosed the problem and walked up the street to buy some engine coolant. After pouring it in, we were able to start the engine. Then he offered to follow me home. When we got there without further trouble, I wanted to pay him for the coolant and for his help. But he refused. "Look," he said, "you're a man of God, and it was a privilege for me to serve you." I was touched and filled with gratitude for this man's kindness. I promised to pray for him and asked his name. "My name is Marvin," he said, "and please pray for my family too."

Wherever you are, Marvin, may God bless you. You not only helped me out in need, but you were Christ to me. You gave me a beautiful lesson in "reaching beyond racial barriers."

But what about being obedient to the Great Commission given by Jesus to the community of disciples at the time of his ascension into heaven? He made it clear that the church does not exist for its own sake. It has a mission, a purpose. In effect, he was saying: "The story of my life, death, and resurrection is good news. Don't let it be forgotten: keep it alive. Tell it the whole world until time is no more" (cf. Mt 28:18-20; Mk 16:15-16). Today we are being reminded that this commission is intended not only for the leaders of the church, but for every one of us. It is no secret that there are millions of people who know little or nothing of Jesus Christ. Or, if they do know him, it makes little practical difference in their lives. They do not experience him as their friend, Savior, and source of strength.

This is why recent popes, and now the American bishops, are calling us to evangelize our world. We Catholics, by and large, are not used to that kind of language. Perhaps it turns us off, because it sounds too much like TV evangelists or the folks who come knocking on our doors demanding to know if we are saved. Or maybe the word evangelize scares us, because we think we are being asked to go door-to-door ourselves to try to convince everyone to become Catholic. No! Evangelization in the Catholic understanding is both simpler and deeper than that. It assumes that most people are like ourselves. They are concerned about health, self-image, relationships, work, family, the meaning of life, and what happens after death. In a word, they are spiritual seekers, even though they may not realize it.

So evangelization really begins not with talking but with listening. Consider this scene, which could happen over the phone, around the kitchen table, at school or work, in the car, at the bowling alley or bar, on the golf course, in the locker room. Somebody starts talking about a problem he or she is having. Instead of giving quick advice or glibly saying to "look on the bright side," you keep listening, maybe ask an occasional question to draw the person out. Only when he or she is finished, do you offer some advice or a word of encouragement. But then you do something else. You say, "You know, I've gone through something like that in my own life. And what helped me most was my faith in God." Then you share briefly what happened to you. And you say, "Maybe you could tell me a bit more about where God is in your life." Or, "Do you ever bring any of this to God in prayer?"

You have now moved the conversation to the spiritual level. Depending on what the person says next, you continue the dialogue. Or, if the person wants to drop it, that's OK, too. In any case, it's a "no-lose" experience. If the other is a committed believer, you have given spiritual encouragement; if the other closes off, you have at least listened with a caring heart and given him or her something to think about. And if the other is an unchurched spiritual seeker, you have tapped into his or her suppressed longing for God and for community. If there is interest, you can follow up with some kind of invitation: "Would you like to talk again?" "I have a good booklet that you might find helpful." "We have a Bible study group that meets every week; would you like to join us next time?" "I know a priest you could talk to about some of the questions you are bringing up." The beauty of this invitational approach is that for most people it is neither coercive nor threatening.

For the last few years I have been involved in teaching and training people in this one-to-one style of evangelizing. I wish you could see the enthusiasm of people as they practice the skills and gain confidence in their ability to listen to others and to share with them their own experience of seeking and finding the action of God in their lives.

The six steps outlined should not be thought of as a fixed sequence, where one step must follow the previous one. But each step will be important on our spiritual journey. Sometimes we will need to pay attention to the dissatisfaction we feel and be alert to the call for a new vision or direction. Other times we will have a decision to make, and we will want to make it in the light of spiritual values. Still other times we will know it's time to take personal inventory because those values have been sliding from our awareness. And, hopefully, the fifth and sixth steps—spending some time in prayer or meditation, and doing something concrete to bring God's healing and love into our corner of the world will become part of our daily behavior pattern.

I want to reiterate what I said in the Preface—that the "masculine" spiritual journey I have traced may well turn out to be a more inclusive "human" journey. After all, the six

Hebrew words for man could have equal application to the spiritual process of women, who also have to deal with their creatureliness, sexuality, need to struggle against opposition, and wounding. Women too are growing toward maturity and toward the wisdom that comes from aging gracefully. As I said in the first chapter, comparing the two journeys would make a fascinating research project.

I am content, though, with offering these reflections for the benefit of the many spiritual men I have come to know, as well as those many others who are seeking a deeper spirituality for their lives. If this book is of any help in their quest, I shall feel richly rewarded.

References

Arnold, Patrick, S.J. 1991. *Wildmen, Warriors and Kings* (Crossroad).*

Barbeau, Clayton. 1982. *Delivering the Male* (Winston).*

Becker, Ernest. 1975. *The Denial of Death* (Macmillian).

Bly, Robert. 1990. *Iron John* (Addison-Weseley).*

Cole, Edwin Louis. 1992. *On Becoming a Real Man.* (Thomas Nelson).*

Covey, Stephen. 1990. *Seven Habits of Highly Effecive People.* (Simon and Schuster).

Goble, Frank G. 1970. *The Third Force: The Psychology of Abraham Maslow* (Grossman).

Erikson, Erik. 1959. "Identity and the Life Cycle" in *Psychological Issues* (Vol. 1, Num. 1).

Habig, Marion, OFM, ed. 1973. "Legend of Perugia" in *St. Francis of Assisi: Omnibus of Sources* (Franciscan Herald Press).

Hays, Edward M. 1979. *Prayers for the Domestic Church: A Handbook of Worship in the Home* (Forest of Peace Publishing).

Hicks, Robert. 1993. *The Masculine Journey* (Navpress).*

Hoare, Liam. 1995. "Sabbath: Time Out to Cultivate the Heart" in *Priestly People* (Newsletter of the Servants of the Paraclete).

Keen, Sam. 1991. *Fire in the Belly* (Bantam Books).*

Kurtz, Ernest, and Katherine Ketcham. 1992. *The Spirituality of Imperfection: Modern Wisdom from Classic Stories* (Bantam Books).

Lazaar, Jonathon. 1992. *Meditations for Men Who Do Too Much* (Simon and Schuster).

Levinson, Daniel. 1978. *The Seasons of a Man's Life* (Ballantine).*

May, Gerald. 1988. *Addiction and Grace* (Harper San Francisco).

May, Rollo. 1969. *Love and Will* (W.W. Norton).

McGann, John. 1996. "Celebrate God's Gift of Sexuality" in *Crux*.

Moore, Robert. 1990. *King, Warrior, Magician, Lover* (Harper San Francisco).*

Nouwen, Henri. 1971. *Creative Ministry* (Doubleday).

O'Neill, Daniel W., ed. 1987. *The New Catholics* (Crossroad).

Pable, Martin, OFM Cap. 1988. *A Man and His God* (Ave Maria Press).*

Peck, M. Scott. 1978. *The Road Less Traveled: A New Psychology of Love, Traditional Values, and Spiritual Growth* (Simon and Schuster).

Rohr, Richard, OFM. 1993. *The Wild Man's Journey* (St. Anthony Messenger Press).*

Sellner, Edward. 1995. *Father and Son* (Ave Maria Press).*

Siegel, Bernie. 1993. *How to Live Between Office Visits* (Harper Collins Publishers).

Smedes, Lewis. 1993. *Shame and Grace* (Harper San Francisco).

Thompson, Keith, ed. 1991. *To Be a Man: In Search of the Deep Masculine* (Jeremy P. Tarcher).*

Trueblood, Elton. 1948. *Alternative to Futility* (Harper).

Walsh, Eugene A. 1977. *The Ministry of the Celebrating Community* (Pastoral Arts Associates of North America).

*The starred works above will be particularly helpful to those who wish to pursue further readings in male spirituality. In addition, they may wish to obtain the following:

Bly, Robert. 1989. "A Gathering of Men." Video of interview with Bill Moyers (PBS).

Pable, Martin. 1994. "Masculine Spirituality." Audio cassettes of a retreat for men (St. Anthony Messenger Press).

Rohr, Richard. 1994. "Fire From Heaven: A Retreat for Men." Audio cassettes (St. Anthony Messenger Press).